Recollections
OF RAVEN AND RICHLANDS
COLONEL CHARLES DAHNMON WHITT

ISBN 978-1-62847-604-0

Recollections of Raven & Richlands

Recollections

Of Raven and Richlands
By
Colonel Charles Dahnmon Whitt

This is a story about growing up in Southwest Virginia, namely Raven, and Richlands, Virginia during the 1940"s – 1960's. It was a much simpler and honest time.

"We thought we were rich, turns out we were; in Discipline, God, and Country standards!"

Includes, "Gone Raven"

Published October 16, 2013
Published by, Dahnmon Whitt Family Publishing
Post Office Box 831
Flatwoods, KY 41139-0831
Phone 606-836-7997
e-mail: c-dahnmon@roadrunner.com
Web Site: to buy books http://dahnmonwhittfamily.com/

Edited By Larry Whitt and Sharon Whitt
Copyright, by Colonel Charles Dahnmon Whitt
All rights reserved, no part of this book may be reproduced or utilized in any form or by any means without the written permission of Colonel Charles Dahnmon Whitt

Colonel Charles Dahnmon Whitt

Chapters   **Page**

Chapter	Page
Dedication	4
Introduction	5
1 The First Place I Remember	29
2 Church and Discipline	41
3 Going to Raven School	50
4 Creeks and Rivers	66
5 Fishing With Uncle Gene	68
6 The First Trout I Ever Caught	73
7 My First Big Trout	79
8 Camping On The Lake	86
9 What Is A Creek	94
10 BB Gun	96
11 Raising Rabbits In Raven	100
12 Nails and Boards	105
13 Fun In Raven	109
14 Aunt Mary Ball Pack and Pappy	123
15 Pete the Parakeet	133
16 Go Fly A Kite	135
17 The N & W and Raven	141
18 Parents and Grandparents	155
19 Son Of A Coal Miner	172

Recollections of Raven & Richlands

Chapter	Page
20 Boy Scouts	174
21 The Raven Super Market	185
22 Richlands High School	195
23 Leaving For The Navy	204
24 Why I Love Raven	213
25 Surnames	218
26 History of Richlands	226
27 Our First Television	244
28 Old Pictures	248
29 Our First Telephone	276
30 Powered Lawnmowers	281
31 S & H Green Stamps	283
32 WRIC Radio	285
33 Air Conditioning	289
34 Killing Hogs	291
35 Busy Richlands	296
36 Haircuts	298
37 Ball Point Pens	300
The Colonel and His Books	301

Colonel Charles Dahnmon Whitt

Dedication

This Book is dedicated to My Father Marvin B. Whitt and all Coal Miners. Also to all the good people that were raised in Raven and Richlands area.

Miner's Memorial, in Richlands, VA

Recollections of Raven & Richlands

Introduction
HISTORY

Raven is an unincorporated community nestled in the Appalachian Mountains of Southwest Virginia. It is situated at the junction of U.S. Route 460 and Virginia 67, and runs along the Clinch River. One side of the Clinch River is embedded with limestone and topped with fertile farming land, whereas the other side is rich in coal veins and abundant timber. These assets supply the major economy for the area with coal being the chief contributor. Raven is served by the Norfolk and Southern Railroad for rail transportation, the Appalachian Power Company for electricity, and General Telephone of the Southwest for telephone service.

Raven derived its name from Frank Raven who worked for a glass company in the Richlands area. Later he moved to the area which now bears his name?

Burbage brought his Union Army through here on a raid to Saltville, Virginia during the Civil War. A group of 300 old men and boys hit them where Raven now is. It was 300 against 8,000 Federals, and was only a slowing tactic to give Saltville time to prepare.

Colonel Charles Dahnmon Whitt

Richlands

Area code(s)

276

FIPS code

51-66928

GNIS feature ID

1473194

Website

http://town.richlands.va.us/

Richlands is a town in Tazewell County, Virginia, United States. The population was 5,823 at the 2010 census. It is part of the Bluefield, WV-VA metropolitan area which has a population of 107,578.

Recollections of Raven & Richlands

History

Located along the banks of the Clinch River, Richlands began as a farming community and was named for its fertile "rich lands".

The Clinch Valley Coal & Iron Company began to develop Richlands in 1890, and company officials hoped Richlands' readily available coal, iron and timber might make it the "Pittsburgh of the South"; the company abandoned its plans following a stock market crash in 1893.

Richlands was incorporated in 1892.

In February 1893, Richlands was the site of a mass lynching of five black railroad workers after it was alleged some of the men had robbed and beat a white man. Four of the railroad workers were arrested and held in the Richlands jail, but the jailor was overpowered by a mob of white townspeople, including

Colonel Charles Dahnmon Whitt

James Hurt, a magistrate and member of Richlands' town council, and James Crabtree, a prominent businessman, who removed the four men and hanged them from the same tree. A fifth black railroad worker was later found and lynched.

The Richlands Historic District encompasses much of downtown Richlands, and the Tazewell Avenue Historic District, and Williams House, are both listed on the National Register of Historic Places.

Geography

Richlands is located at

37°5'40"N 81°48'22"W (37.094444, -81.806060)
According to the United States Census Bureau, the town has a total area of 2.7 square miles (6.9 km²), all land.

Demographics

As of the census of 2010, there were 5,823 people, 2,552 households, and 1,632 families residing in the town. The population density was 1,565.7 people per square mile (603.8/km²). There were 2,137 housing units at an average density of 807.4 per square mile (311.4/km²). The racial makeup of the town was 98.75% White, 0.05% African American, 0.12% Native American, 0.51% Asian, 0.19% from other races, and 0.39% from two or more races. Hispanic or Latino of any race were 0.34% of the population.

Colonel Charles Dahnmon Whitt

There were 1,882 households out of which 25.2% had children under the age of 18 living with them, 48.7% were married couples living together, 12.8% had a female householder with no husband present, and 35.0% were non-families. 32.1% of all households were made up of individuals and 15.6% had someone living alone who was 65 years of age or older. The average household size was 2.20 and the average family size was 2.76.

In the town the population was spread out with 20.1% under the age of 18, 8.3% from 18 to 24, 27.7% from 25 to 44, 25.4% from 45 to 64, and 18.5% who were 65 years of age or older. The median age was 41 years. For every 100 females there were 81.9 males. For every 100 females age 18 and over, there were 79.0 males.

The median income for a household in the town was $23,712, and the median income for a family was $30,257. Males had a median income of $30,682 versus $18,670 for females. The per capita income for the town was $15,548. About 13.6% of families and 17.8% of the population were below the poverty line, including 24.1% of those under age 18 and 16.9% of those age 65 or over.

Education

Richlands is served by the Tazewell County Public School System. Schools in Richland include:

Richlands Elementary School

Richlands Middle School

Richlands High School

The Southwest Virginia Community College is located in Richlands.

The Collage is actually on Route 19 between Claypool Hill and Belfast

Colonel Charles Dahnmon Whitt

Raven School

Raven Elementary School serves the people of the extreme western area of Tazewell County. The school, which was originally located in the area called "School House Hill", now occupies a more accessible tract of land located in Doran Bottom. Since relocating the school has progressed from a building with five classrooms to a school plant that is now composed of twenty-five classrooms, a library media center, a cafeteria, office space, and the newest addition, a spacious gymnasium, which is used by the community as well as the student body.

Raven is located at:

37□°05 '21□ N 81□°51 '22□ W (37.089046, -81.855993). According to the United States Census Bureau, the CDP has a total area of 6.8 square miles (17.7 km), all land.

Recollections of Raven & Richlands

Demographics

As of the census of 2000, there were 2,593 people, 1,064 households, and 774 families residing in the CDP. The population density was 379.5 people per square mile (146.6/km²). There were 1,219 housing units at an average density of 178.4/sq mi (68.9/km). The racial makeup of the CDP was 99.04% White, 0.04% African American, 0.08% Native American, and 0.85% from two or more races. Hispanic or Latino of any race was 0.77% of the population.

There were 1,064 households out of which 30.6% had children under the age of 18 living with them, 55.5% were married couples living together, 13.1% had a female householder with no husband present, and 27.2% were non-families. 24.4% of all households were made up of individuals and 11.7% had someone living alone who was 65 years of age or older. The average household size was 2.44 and the average family size was 2.88.

Colonel Charles Dahnmon Whitt

In the CDP the population was spread out with 23.1% under the age of 18, 9.1% from 18 to 24, 28.8% from 25 to 44, 26.3% from 45 to 64, and 12.6% who were 65 years of age or older. The median age was 37 years. For every 100 females there were 94.5 males. For every 100 females age 18 and over, there were 91.1 males.

The median income for a household in the CDP was $19,104, and the median income for a family was $22,891. Males had a median income of $23,080 versus $19,327 for females. The per capita income for the CDP was $10,356. About 16.0% of families and 19.7% of the population were below the poverty line, including 25.6% of those under age 18 and 24.7% of those ages 65 or over.

Raven is a census-designated place (CDP) in Russell and Tazewell counties in the U.S. State of Virginia. The population was 2,593 at the 2000 census.

Recollections of Raven & Richlands

This is a well-known photograph titled "Coal Camp, near Raven, VA, 1970".

Colonel Charles Dahnmon Whitt

By: Builder Levy

I first viewed this picture (while attending Marshall University) in 1994 in Levy's book "Images of Appalachian Coalfields" in the Renaissance bookstore/coffeehouse in Huntington, WV. I recall just staring at it for several minutes, then walking around the bookstore, then coming back and picking up the book and studying the scene a little more, because it captured in a poetic way the melancholy feel of the coal camps that I recalled riding through with my father as a kid. As essential as the row of old company houses, the dusty road, and the choked stream are to the photo. I feel that the most important element in the photograph is the cloud suspended above the hollow. I don't know whether it is mountain fog, smoke from the coal stoves in the homes, or pollution from what looks like a slate dump in the background. Perhaps it is all three swirled together. Later I found Builder's "Images" book at the Raleigh County Library and checked it out several times. Of course every picture in that book is great, but this one is still my favorite. It captured my imagination, and was one of the things that inspired me to get out and take some "coal camp" pictures of my own. Interestingly I asked Builder Levy where this particular coal camp "near Grundy"(Close to Raven and Richlands) was and he said that it was between Grundy and Raven along U.S. Route 460. However, he also said that the little village has since vanished, possibly due to flooding or highway expansion. But, fortunately, the coal camp has been immortalized and has been an inspiration to me and probably others, because Builder decided to pull over on U.S. Route 460 and take this picture nearly four decades ago. (Photo courtesy of Builder Levy - used with permission)

This is the Raven School; I went here for the 4th Grade, the first year it opened. I went back in the 7th Grade.

Many rooms and improvements have been added over the years.

Colonel Charles Dahnmon Whitt

Another picture of the Premier, Virginia coal camp, as it looked in 1974. (Photo by Jack Corn, courtesy of, The U.S. National Archives)

Recollections of Raven & Richlands

Miners have been working, coal is going out!

Notice the old automobiles, and also that the train has N & W on them. The N & W has not been in existence for years. It is now part of the Norfolk Southern Railroad after a merger.

The Miner's Company Store.

Recollections of Raven & Richlands

The old

Raven Red Ash Coal Company

Colonel Charles Dahnmon Whitt

"Lake Park" in Richlands. I learned to swim here. It was drained many years ago.

Recollections of Raven & Richlands

"Library"
**Know what this little building is used for?
Some call it a JOHN!**

Colonel Charles Dahnmon Whitt

The Author in 1944
Colonel Charles Dahnmon Whitt Sr.

Recollections of Raven & Richlands

"Miners walking home after a hard day underground."

Colonel Charles Dahnmon Whitt

This is the Everett Fleming Family in Red Ash before he moved to Stinson Bottom. (About 1947)

Front Row: Me the Author is the baby held my Cousin Nancy, Cousin Phyllis, Cousin Jimmy, Brother Larry, behind Larry is Brother Jerry, Cousin Doris,

Second Row: Grandpa Everett Fleming, Thelma my Aunt, Grandma Lura Bellamy Fleming, Cousin Clara, My mother Edith Lyle Fleming Whitt, Cousin Betty. Back Row: Tilden Thacker and Elmer Hooker.

Recollections of Raven & Richlands

Red Ash School

Colonel Charles Dahnmon Whitt

Raven Red Ash Works and Camp

Chapter 1
The First Place I Remember

The first place I remember in my life is Raven, Virginia. I hear I was not born here but in the Clinch Valley Clinic in nearby Richlands, Virginia. I was born in the hospital instead of at home because of complications.

I was told that we lived in Richlands when I was born. The family moved to the main part of Raven (The Main Drag) so to speak early in 1945. The house was behind the building that housed Cap Justice's Beer Joint and the upstairs was used for the Coal Miner's Union and school.

.Then we moved up on Road Ridge, (The Old Kentucky Turnpike) to a small farm right on top of the ridge. Most that I know about that is what I was told by my family.

The house on the farm was without electricity and indoor plumbing. My dad was a coal miner and Jack of all trades. Because the wind blew all the time on the ridge, Dad got the idea of a windmill. He set up a wind driven generator and back-up car battery system to give us lights. Dad strung little 6 volt car lights all over the house and we had light. I heard that dad first put the windmill on top of the house but it shook and made too much noise. The he moved it to the garage and the problem was corrected.

Also on the farm we had a horse, a cow, bunches of chickens and a dog. The cow gave us milk and the chickens our eggs. Mom churned the butter and she loved the cream, so she gained a lot of weight while on the farm. Now all of this is just hearsay from the stories my family told me. I do know about the windmill because Dad had it after we moved down to Stinson Bottom in Raven.

Now back to the first place I remember, it was the house in Stinson Bottom. It was not the West Raven as so many called it. There was an old White Church at the top of the hill on Route 67 and to the right was West Raven, to the left led to Stinson Bottom. Then it went on and crossed Mill Creek and then on down by the N & W railroad and the Clinch River. You could follow it on to Simmons Town and cross over into Russell County to Long Branch.

Dad bought the house in Stinson Bottom, as unfinished. It only had a sub floor and tar paper siding when we got there. It was a nice lot on high ground with a gentle slope to the creek and bordered the dirt road on the side and on the front.

Another story I heard Mom tell many times was about our cat, a big white cat called, "Puss." Now living near the creek; the rats came calling and Puss made short work of them, in a short time the rats were gone. Mom said the cracks in the sub floor were so big that Puss would reach down and pull up a rat with her claws and kill it instantly.

Of course the house was much improved as I remember it. Dad had put in electricity and running water after a while. I remember getting my weekly bath in a big round tin tub. My brothers Jerry and Larry had carried water from a nice spring for some time before Dad and my Grandfather Everett Fleming dug a well on the property line.

I am not sure when or how it came about but Grandpa Everett Fleming and Grandma Lura bought the lot next to us. Grandpa and Dad, Marvin Whitt got together and drilled a well on the line, it worked out well as there was plenty of water 40 feet down to supply both families. There was one draw-back; it had natural gas in the well.

Colonel Charles Dahnmon Whitt

I had learned to love this place by the time I could get out and play with my neighbor kids. There were four or five families in the near vicinity with children and more from nearby West Raven.
There were many things about, that would interest a young boy of that era.

We had big hills I called mountains, we had a creek, we had a river, we had a field to play on, and we had big rocks under some fine oak trees to sit under and plot out the fun.

Living in Raven was a fun place. As I began to put things in my memory bank I knew I loved Raven.
We had good neighbors, yet none were (in our face) close.

They all had kids and we all played together as soon as I was big enough. Jerry and Larry already played and enjoyed the Stinson Bottom.

It has been some fifty years now, so I will name some of the families, Shelton, Kennedy, Johnson, Joyce, Hodge, Lambert, Cordle, and Farmer.

Some of the families moved or had more children over time. Of course West Raven was near and we had friends there also, Reedy, Welch, Grose, Horton, Webb, Lawson, Webb, and many more.

This is the Old White Church, (Raven Methodist South) and also the Red Men's Lodge in the upper story. This is a group of Red Men in front of the church.

This is the Old White Church, (Raven Methodist) Picture taken (most likely) by Charles H. Whitt in1910

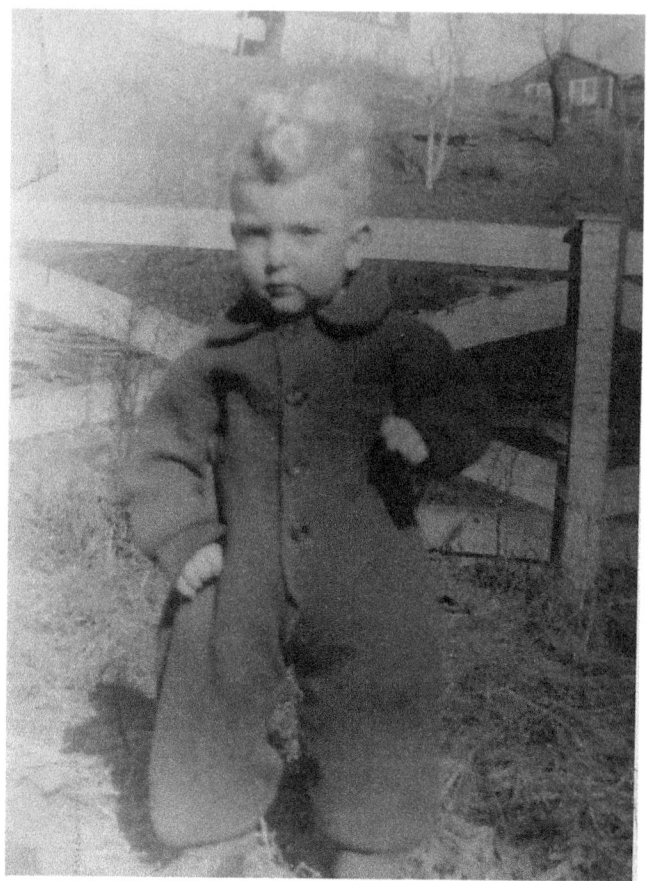

Dahnmon at about 1946, Red Ash Virginia

Brothers, Larry and Jerry at an early age.

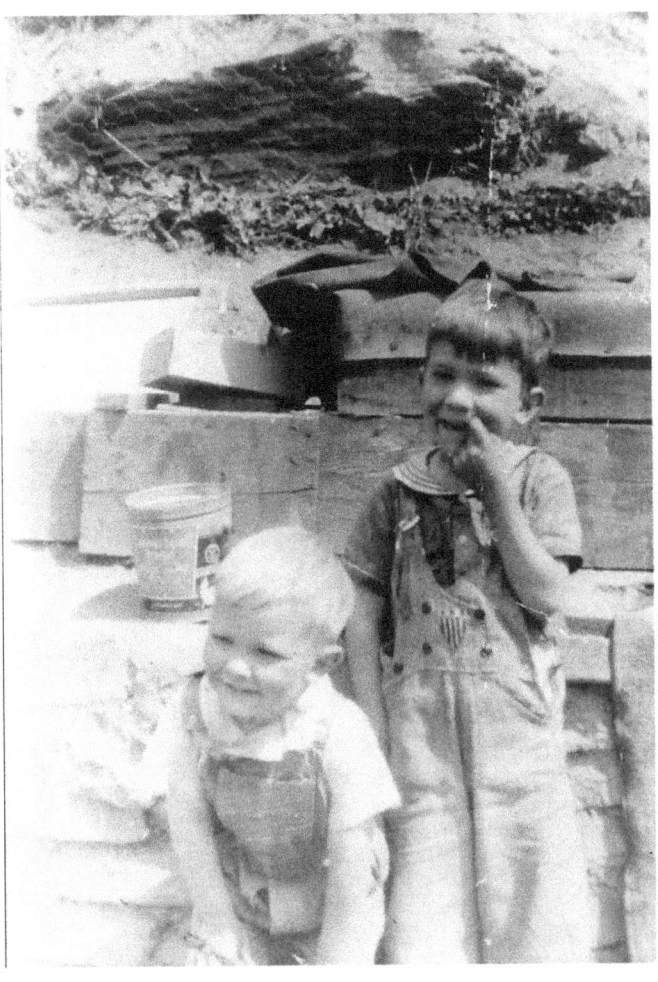

A rare trip to Camden Park, Kenova, WV.
I am the runt in front, Jerry to the left, Larry to the right, and Dad Marvin and Mom Edith.
About 1948 or 1949

Colonel Charles Dahnmon Whitt

**Dahnmon on Road Ridge, near Raven
About 1946**

My Grandparents: Joseph Everett Fleming and Lura Elizabeth Bellamy Fleming before 1951

Colonel Charles Dahnmon Whitt

**My Grandpa, Charles Henry Whitt
About 1950**

Chapter 2
Church and Discipline

My first memories of church were going to the Raven Methodist Church. (Old White Church)

It was the big wooden two story church that is in the prior photo. The Red Men's Lodge and The Odd Fellows was in the upper story while the bottom was our church.

Both of my Grandpas were members of the Red Men and the Odd Fellows as well as sometime in their life belonged to the Klu Klux Klan.

I was told by my family that back in the day the KKK was necessary to take care of the un-Godly people like husbands that would not take care of their family. The Klan would leave a bundle of switches on the door step as a warning. It the bad husband did not snap too, the KKK would take him out behind the barn and give him a good "whooping." Many folks think that the KKK was just to keep black folks straight, not the case.

Grandpa Whitt lived right behind the Old White Church and served as a custodian for the Lodge a time.

Colonel Charles Dahnmon Whitt

I don't know too much about the Red Man Lodge, but they had the letters in a big sign high up on the front of the church that read F L T. We boys heard it meant Faithful, Loyal, and True, But the bigger boys told me it stood for Fat Ladies Titties, or Fleas, Lice, and Ticks, or Fools, Liars, and Thieves. We would all snicker and laugh at all the sayings.

I went to services at the Raven Methodist Church over the years. It had two doors in front. When it was built, before 1900, the Methodist had an idea that the ladies needed a door and the gentlemen also needed a door. That is no longer thought in the more modern traditions. Now all the years I went there we all used the same door or both of them in warm weather.

The Old Church had big windows that could be opened in hot weather. There was no such thing as air conditioning in the hills of Virginia in the 1950's.

Now for heat we had the biggest pot-bellied stove I ever remember seeing. It was near the front but centered in the left hand side section of pews. On cold days, the old stove was fired up with wood and then banked with coal. It would glow cherry red at times. It did not give the best comfort, as when you faced it your face would burn, yet your back side would be cold.

The pews were long and made of wood. They were made to keep folks awake I think because there was not much comfort afforded by them.

The restroom was a path to the John.

The main thing I remember about the Old White Church was that the Bible was taught and the gospel of Christ was preached there. It was pastored by many pastors as to the true Methodist methods of the time, the pastors were moved frequently.

Another thing I learned there was that the Holy Spirit abided there in the hearts of the good mountain people.

When Dad and Mom decided to join the church at Raven Methodist, I was small but I do remember it to this day. Dad and Mom went to the front to take their vows. I did not want to be left out! Guess what, I was right there with them and gave everyone a surprise. I was not sent back to my pew, I joined that day also. I am not too sure but I think I was baptized that day in the old Methodist tradition, sprinkled. (I have been baptized two times since, in the Clinch, and once by the Baptist in Tennessee.)

Another thing I wanted to mention was the deal I had with Dad. You see after a time I was big enough to go fishing with friends, but in order to go I promised to go to church first.

The other boys and I would sit near the back for a quick escape as soon as the closing prayer was offered. Now we had this old retired saint, Preacher Gibson, which was almost always called on to pray us out of the service. We boys would be standing and holding on to the top of the pew in front of us ready to run. Preacher Gibson was the slowest praying man I have ever heard. About the time you thought he would say amen, he would pause and think up more stuff to pray about and take off again, our knuckles would be white because of the grip we held on the pew. Finally we would get the "Amen" and out the door we went. It is a good thing no one was starting in, we would have run over them.

I am amazed today of the knowledge of the Bible and the good rules I learned at that old church. We were raised up right and even though we did depart from it, most of us have turned out to be good people.

I also want to say that most of the parents in and around Raven were God fearing folks. These good people taught the "Golden Rule", God, and country to their children.

If you don't know the Golden Rule it is taken from the Bible. It basically says, "Do unto Others as You Would Have Them do unto you."
The Golden Rule applied to a lot of subjects, no lying, no cheating, no fighting, no stealing, and no sassing. If the rules were broken, it brought quick judgment and also quick correction.

All of this was backed up at school and home by the "Board of Education, (paddle) at school and by the hand or even a belt at home. If a child got a paddling at school, that meant they got a spanking at home as well.

I can remember Mom saying to me when she had to spank me, "This hurts me more than it hurts you." I never could figure that one out because a spanking always hurt my behind pretty bad.

I remember another lesson I learned at an early age, was not to argue with older people. My Grandma Lura would get things mixed up from time to time; I would try to correct her. Dad heard this and pulled me to the side and used his firm voice. "Don't you ever argue with Grandma, even if she says something is white and it is black? That is sassing and disrespectful."

I got the point and was careful what I said to Grandma Lura after that. She was such a sweet old woman that deserved respect from all people.

Recollections of Raven & Richlands

Grandpa Fleming's House.
**Me and Linda, my first little friend
This was before I started school.**

Dahnmon in Humble Beginnings

A typical class at the Old Raven School
Remembered by Jerry Davis

Chapter 3
Going to Raven School

As primitive as the Raven school was, it was a great learning facility. Learning the three R's was not the only thing we learned. We learned discipline, God, and country.

I am guessing it was the summer of 1951 that Mom took me to the Old School on School House Hill to register for school and get shots and a physical. The Old school was on Red Root Ridge up above Raven Town. We were there all together, all the new kids and I. It was kinda scary, and some of the kids cried. I think most of us had a fear of the unknown.

My birthdate didn't fall just right to get me in early. I was born in September so I was almost seven years old before I started school.

We did not have kindergarten in 1951, so I didn't know any letters or numbers, let alone know any reading. I found out during the next few months that Dick and Jane would help teach me to read. For you modern folks, Dick and Jane were in my first grade reader. I know that today little four year olds are learning all the basic stuff.

Now during this time and just before I had been sick a lot. I had rheumatic fever and about everything else I could catch. I was not prepared for school and had a fear of it.

My best friend Bertina was a playmate of mine, she was my first real sweetheart, and lived close to us. We were buddies and our moms would take turns taking us to and from school. This was a big help, At least I knew somebody in this strange situation.

Colonel Charles Dahnmon Whitt

Best Seller in 1950

This was my little buddy, Bertina Shelton, My first few years in Raven. She is still a dear friend.

Colonel Charles Dahnmon Whitt

Now Tazewell County School Board must have been mighty poor as to having buildings and money to run the schools on. They had rented the United Mine Workers Hall for our class. It was up some steep steps to the second floor of Cap Justices' beer joint. Of course the union meetings were at night as well as most of the beer drinking so we were not bothered by that. It was not the best of situations to have first graders there.

I remember the restroom facilities were out in a small lot behind the building; most likely the beer drinkers used it as well. It was just a path and a common outhouse. One thing I remember about that old out house was the day I dropped my nice leather cap with the ear muffs right in the hole. It was laying down there looking up at me as if to say, "Get me out of this this nasty." I ran up the long course of steps and told my teacher of my misfortune, she got a coat hanger and gave it to me. I was to fish it out, but once I hooked it and pulled it up I could see how nasty and stinky it was, I shook it off the hook. I told a fib to my teacher and mom. I said, I couldn't get it out.

I remember one part of school where we were going to learn about numbers. The teacher, Miss Hale, had a good plan to teach us. She was bringing cans and other items and we were going to put a price tax on them and play store. That is one time I got sick and missed a lot of school. I was really looking forward to playing "Store".

Now between being sick and missing so much school I don't remember just what happened from first to third grades. Evidently I was promoted to second grade even though I was not ready.

My teachers in the Raven School were;
1. **Miss Hale**
2. **Miss Nichols & Mrs. Ball**
3. **Miss Presley**
4. **Miss Boyd**
5. **Miss Meadows**
6. **Miss Billie Sue Beavers**
7. **Miss Westall**

Now we have a Raven School reunion every 4th weekend in July for anyone that wants to come, old or young.

School Year 1954-1955

**Dahnmon in first grade.
1950-1951**

Colonel Charles Dahnmon Whitt

I remember the next fall I was a big kid and walked the long way to school with many of my friends. I met another little girl that liked to carry my lunch kit. I let her. Her name was Susie Lambert.

I thought things were going pretty good, we had learned enough about our letters and we started writing I love you letters to each other. We were having our pledge to the flag and a Bible story every morning and I thought I was doing well. I even remember drawing a groundhog and the teacher showed it to Mister Rondo Ball, our principal. They all agreed I was on my way to becoming a great artist.

I was in the second grade long enough to get into some mischief. Now it was just fun two other boys and I was doing. Miss Knuckles, our teacher, was out of the room and Mr. Ball caught us chasing each other with a broom. He brought the "Board of Education," with him, (paddle). Miss Knuckles came in and he told her of our great mischief. He asked her if he could correct us. She agreed but the look on her face showed pity for us. All three of us were bent over and the paddle was put to use on our posterior. My butt was on fire. I found out later he was not famous for sparing the paddle.

Recollections of Raven & Richlands

They all must have forgotten how good I was, because before I knew it I was back down in Raven in the union hall again. My teacher there was Mrs. Ball, the wife of the principal. Was I back in the first grade or was I just getting a refresher course? I must have been put back because all of my cool friends were now a grade ahead of me.

Now I was struck again, I came down with spinal meningitis, and got really sick. I had high fever and was out of my head. The churches all around prayed for me. God was not through with me. I remember getting a yellow fluid in the muscle of both of my upper legs. It hurt really bad and I cried. I have since learned that they gave me sulfa drugs as they did not have modern medicines in the early 1950's. Dad told me later that it had affected my kidneys and I missed more school. You see mom and dad had lost the last baby, Joe Ed, to whooping cough and were being extra careful with me. I finally made it to the third grade and my teacher, Miss Presley, claimed to be kin to Elvis, so this must have been about the time he started getting famous.

The second grade through seventh grade went to the ancient old school up on the hill above Raven town until the new school was built in Doran Bottom. The building was old when I went there; even my Dad had gone there in the twenties.

The old building was made of brick and by the 1950's there were many loose brick. The floors were made of wood and had been oiled to make them last. It had big windows that you could open in warm weather. The windows were loose and in the fall we had to contend with wasps that had made themselves a summer home there.

The heating system was a big potbellied stove in each room. No one thought much about it, but the building was a fire hazard. The oiled floors and the hot stoves could be a disaster. One morning when I got to school the janitor had been fixing the fires for the day and a hot ember jumped out on the floor. It took off in a blaze. Just so happened he had the drinking water container nearby with 5 gallons of water. He got it put out real quick. I stood there and watched the frantic man move in a hurried manner.

Speaking of drinking water, we had to fill the little tin barrels each day to have drinking water in the room.

The rest room facilities were out back of the school. . They were outside Johns. There was no grass, but the school yard had plenty of gravel. One thing I thought was great was all the giant oak trees that were around the far reaches of the school ground.

We had the old-time desks, where you sit on the seat and the top of the desk was the back part to the next student's seat.

I must mention that even though we had a primitive school, we had discipline, and a good place to learn. Our teachers were dedicated to teaching us. We kids at the Raven school were quite happy, we didn't know any difference. Many of the kids that went through Raven school went on to excel in further education and many became professional people. Even the more average kids got an education that would serve them all of their lives. My dad went to Raven School and never went to high school. He ran a mining business and many folks thought he had a college education.

Our House in Raven
Dahnmon in 1955

Recollections of Raven & Richlands

How did we get to school? We walked to school; we had no big yellow buses at that time. Now from my home I had a good walk. I took the shortest way by heading out the lane towards the Clinch River and the N & W railroad. I followed the railroad to the Raven Depot, and turned left to go through the entire length of town. I got so good at walking the rails I could stay on a rail the entire quarter mile.

After walking to the end of town I crossed over and started the long walk up the hill. I walked for about a quarter of a mile to a curve and turned back the other direction. The curve was sort of like a switch back. After about another quarter of mile all uphill I would arrive at school. It was a good two mile walk to school with half of it up hill.

We kids had a lot of fun walking together and playing on the way. Sometimes there would be a bully or a prankster, but we all dealt with them in stride. We were like a herd of turtles going to school, but when school was out we had to march in single file off the hill to the bottom and there we went our separate ways.

As for dinner we carried a lunch pail or brown bag. You should have seen the diverse food we carried. Some brought left-overs from supper while others brought sandwiches. No one made fun of any ones food or clothes.

The one thing I remember about school is that it started with a pledge to the flag, then a prayer, and in most cases we got to listen to a Bible story.

There was never a threat of a bomb or someone coming to shoot up the place. We were taught the love of God and the love of our country. We were taught the Golden Rule and we lived by it. If anyone strayed they would get the "Board Of Education" across their butts.

Things changed in the late fifties on into the early sixties. We got a new school building across the Clinch River over in the Doran Bottom. The school was only half as big as we needed. At first the children were divided, some went to the old school while some went to the new one. Next came the closing of the Old School House. Then the school system started the stagger system which meant there were two shifts. There was a morning class and an evening class. This made for shorter days which suited me just fine.

When the new school opened it brought on the big yellow school busses.

Recollections of Raven & Richlands

Sad Times, May 1951 Grandpa Everett Fleming died.
Clinch Valley Memorial Cemetery
This is Grandma Lura and Mom Edith at his grave in Richlands, way to the back is the Clinch Valley Clinic Notice the old car, I think a 1947 Ford.

Chapter 4
Creeks and Rivers

My story about growing up in Raven would not be complete without mentioning the creeks and rivers in the area.

Mill Creek was right on the back of our property and it had a lot to do with my youth. It was a wonderful place to play and learn things. I had a great fascination with Mill Creek, and I was drawn to it, even though I was told to stay out of it.

Of course the bigger Clinch River was the next place I wanted to be around. It was nearby and I had to grow up some before I could go there, unless an adult took me. I was always ready to go.

The Clinch offered pretty good fishing and as I became bigger, I even swam in its waters. My second baptism took place there as my Scout Master W.W. Smith told me I needed to be baptized in running water and dunked all the way under.

Other creeks and rivers in the area were also important places to a boy in the 1950's and 60's. Clear Fork, Big and Little Tumbling, Wolf Creek, Cedar Creek and others were great trout streams.

One other thing I wanted to mention about Mill Creek was how it got its name. There is a beautiful creek falls just up the creek from where I lived. At one time there was a mill there and once when Tazewell County changed it boundaries, the mill was a focal point. The line between Russell and Tazewell intersect at the falls.

Chapter 5
Fishing With Uncle Gene

When I was around eight years of age, My Uncle David Eugene took an interest in my fishing education. I was all for the new experience, and learned the love of fishing.

At the back of our home place, God put a creek. It was called Mill Creek, because at one time there was a grist mill at the base of a natural water falls. About one quarter of a mile down the little creek it ran into the Clinch River. This creek became a place of many hours of pleasure for me as I grew up. Above the creek on the other side was a steep hill, we called it a mountain when I was a kid. It was also a place of adventure, I may tell about it in a later tale.

Just at the corner of Dad's lots on the upstream side were the dirt and gravel road and a bridge that crossed Mill Creek. This was the first place I dropped a worm that I can remember. There was mostly Creek Minnows (I called them Minners) in it, but in the spring the Horny Heads migrated up stream to lay eggs I reckon. At any rate the big minnow like fish, with little knots on their heads, was headed up Mill Creek. When I said big, I meant big for minnows. It was fun to catch the shaking things.

Uncle Gene came and we got some garden worms and went way down the creek close to the Clinch that first time. The creek made a good turn and there was a hole against the bank. The creek was only eight to ten feet wide at this section. Gene baited up the little hook and tossed it over in the moving water and something took off with it. Gene gave a quick jerk and missed the little fish, but he caught its lips. We looked at the bare hook that had little fishy lips hanging on it. We laughed at the site, and Uncle Gene said, "Guess I jerked a little hard!"

We went fishing several times that summer, as time went by. I was introduced to seining and crawdad catching. I learned about hellgrammites the wormy little creature with a bunch of legs and a deadly pincher on the front end. Uncle Gene said, "They are good for small mouth bass, guess they turn into some kind of bug when they grow up and get out of the water."

I also learned about the sneaky snakes that played in the creek and even in the river. I learned about the plant that loved the banks of creeks and rivers in Virginia. You guessed it, Poison Oak, that green three leafed devil plant that loved to make blisters on unsuspecting boys like me. Yes, I got a good dose of it that summer. I learned to look for the hateful stuff.

Before the summer was gone we had gone to the Clinch many times, fishing with worms, minnows, crawdad tails, and oh yes hellgrammites. I was afraid of the twisty, pinching, "Hellesimites," as I called them. I found out my favorite fish to catch was the vicious little fighter, the Red Eye. If they were to grow to ten pounds a feller just couldn't land one. They were so aggressive, tearing worms from the hook and almost yanking the little green sapling from my hands.

When we got back with the fish, I had to help clean the fish. This was not much fun as they were slick, scaled and had guts you had to cut out. They also had prickly spines in their fins that loved to stick you when you tried to hold them.

Sometimes we would go seining at the creek falls which had a natural trough at the bottom, and the minnows were usually thick in this two feet of water. One day Uncle Gene sat the burlap seine at one end and I was supposed to wade while thrashing and making a commotion to scare the Minners into the seine. Only thing, there was a snake hanging on the falls sticking its head right at me. No way was I going to scare minnows when that thing was there. Uncle Gene pleaded while being bent over holding the seine.

"Come on Dahnmon, scare the Minners this way," he said.

"I ain't going to do it!" I answered.

Uncle Gene stood up and took a handle of the seine and hit at that old creek snake and it swam right in front of me to the deeper hole to my left and on down the creek.

Uncle Gene was a patient young man, but he was a little exasperated after that.

"Now are you going to scare the minners to me?" he asked.

I waded on into the hole shifting my feet and dancing my way right up to the seine. Uncle Gene raised the burlap sack trap and we had a bunch of the little fishes we call minners. Red Eyes and small mouth bass love the little minnows.

I never caught any whoppers with Uncle Gene, but I did

Colonel Charles Dahnmon Whitt

learn a lot about fishing and baiting and even cleaning fish. I learned about being around water and the great outdoors around my home in Tazewell County, Va. Mill Creek, and the Clinch River held many adventures back in the early fifties. I learned names like the Curve, Dixon Hole, and the Bridge, (N & W Railroad Bridge, crossed Mill Creek as it ran beside the Clinch River) the Swinging Bridge, and the Red Eye Hole.

One other thing I learned, or maybe it came natural like, I learned to tell fish stories.

I think Uncle Gene was back from the Army and taking the summer off before he tied himself down to anything. Dad worked every day at the mine and Gene was free to fish that summer. He has always been my favorite Uncle, and I made a lot of memories that summer. Funny thing was I did not like to eat the fish we caught. I love fish today, and love Uncle Gene.

Chapter 6
The First Trout I Ever Caught

I remember it like it was yesterday, that first wiggly Trout I had in my slick hands. It all started the year before when I was a first grader. Trout season opened in western Virginia at noon in early April. Back then people in the area would take off work to enjoy the stocked mountain streams in the western counties. My Dad did not miss work very much but he must have really enjoyed the annual opening day of trout season. I remember as he prepared to go fishing that day, I wanted to go with him so bad. He knew the mountain terrain and rugged trout streams were not the place for a first grader on opening day. Even though I put up a demanding performance of tears and pleading I was left behind. Dad did halfway promise that I could go the next year.

Dad left with his store bought cane pole and seemed to be gone forever. I waited with great anticipation for his return, because I knew he would have some of the beautiful Rainbow Trout for me to look at and even eat, even though I did not like fish too much.

Sure enough when Dad got home he had three of the most beautiful fish I ever saw. I remember them as

Colonel Charles Dahnmon Whitt

really big, but like everything else, things are big to a first grader. I was so proud of Dad's accomplishment, and just knew I could catch some if I just had a chance.

Back to my fish story, Dad did let me go when I was in the second grade. It was a beautiful spring day as I remember it. I was all excited and had my little green pole that Dad cut from the brush along the way. He attached the black fishing line about half way down the pole. Then he tied it again at the very top of the green sapling. He explained that if a fish broke my pole he would still be tied at the center. Dad was very smart like that.

Dad packed us some sandwiches and stuff in a brown bag, got our night crawlers, and we headed for Wolf Creek. This is some of the most rugged country in Virginia.

Dad told me to be really careful because of the rough conditions, but I thought I was a tough boy in the second grade. When we got to Wolf Creek Dad let me fish by myself, but he stayed close so he could do a rescue if he needed to.

The little leafs were just starting to grow and the

mountain Dogwoods were blooming. There was much greenery even this early in the spring due to the Mountain Laurel, and Hemlocks. The rocks were so slick, as if God had given them a greasing. As soon as we left the car I started a trend for the day, fall down and get up. Dad thought it was funny, but still was afraid I would get hurt.

"Now Son, be careful, if you get hurt we will have to go home," Dad said.

I had what they call fisherman's luck, *"A wet tail and a hungry gut."*

Now back then the season did not open until twelve noon, so we all got our tackle ready, and had a bite to eat. Then we put on a night crawler and waited for the magical hour to drop our baits to the awaiting trout. The game wardens were walking up and down the banks disguised as fishermen trying to catch somebody dropping a hook in too early. They wore fishing clothes and had flies on their hats. Dad pointed them out to me and warned me not to start too early. He said to watch him, and when he started fishing for me to start also. I could hardly wait.

Finally we were fishing in earnest along with about

every other men and boys in the western end of Virginia. People were getting their lines tangled with each other, and some were slipping and sliding almost as much as me.

People started yanking out the flopping fish and I even got a bite or two. I was too slow to hook the sneaky things. Dad had three or four nice trout and I still had not caught my first.

I did the forbidden thing in fishing, I moved in on two fellows that were having really good luck. They gave me a dirty look but didn't say anything. I baited up and flipped my worm out among the hungry trout and sure enough one wanted it. I yanked on the little green pole and the trout landed right in my hands against my chest. The wrestling match was on as I tried to hold on to the slippery Rainbow Trout. As I remember it, it was a big one, but I lost the battle, it was free once again in Wolf Creek.

I was exasperated at giving my prized catch its freedom, and just stood there for a long moment. I remember I started to trudge to the bank to get another worm, but one of the fishermen gave me another worm so I would just be still. I didn't get another fish that year, but I felt some comfort in knowing I had a whopper in my hands. Remember what I said about things looking big when you are a kid!

The day went fast and it was time to go home. Dad had six nice sized fish and we headed to the car. I was totally worn out after fighting the rough ground, slick rocks and a whopper trout. Dad consoled me and said there would be other trips. He explained that I needed a landing net, even though he had none of his own. Sure enough the next year came and I was there with my new landing net. Guess what, I caught not one but two. Dad and I never missed an opening day of trout season until I left for the Navy.

Colonel Charles Dahnmon Whitt

See our favorite meeting place in the back ground

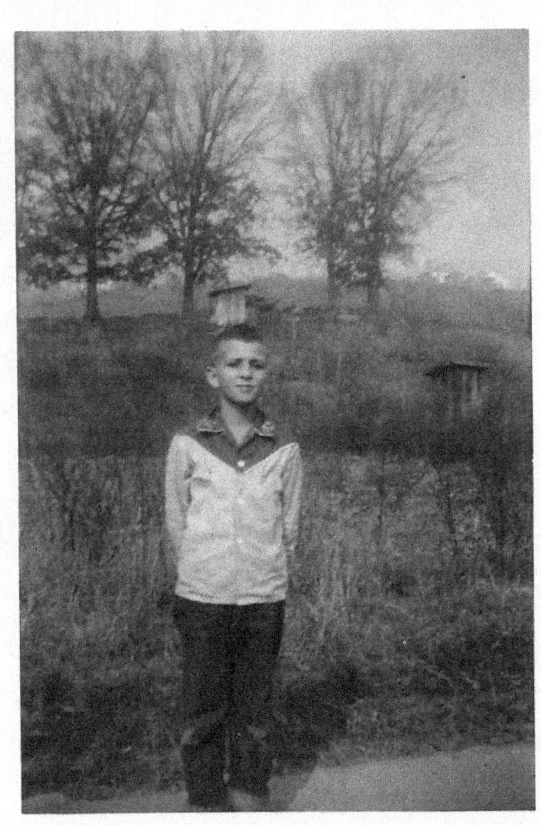

the rocks under the trees up on the hill. Notice all the out-door Johns.

Recollections of Raven & Richlands

Chapter 7
My First Big Trout

Once upon a time when I was around fourteen I had a covenant with Dad! I could go fishing on Sunday afternoon with Doug and his Grand Paw John, after I got out of church. I always made it a point to go to The Raven Methodist Church where Dad was the Sunday school Superintendent and Lay Leader. He thought it to be important for me to be in church every Sunday. I thought it was very important for me to go fishing with John and Doug most every Sunday. So we came to an understanding, I went to church and John would pick up Doug and myself shortly thereafter.

John was a coal miner and loved the weekend. He was one of the most proficient fishermen I ever knew. If only one fish was caught, you could bet John would be the one that did the catching. He would take Doug and I and head out to Little Tumbling Creek, Little River, Cedar Creek, Clear Fork and numerous other mountain streams in southwest Virginia.

This beautiful summer day, Eugene, Doug's daddy decided to go and wet a line with us. We hurriedly got our tackle together and got into John's Red 1957 four door hardtop Chevy and traveled through the beautiful countryside of Tazewell County. We made small talk about this and that, and before long we were crossing the little woodland bridge over Little Tumbling Creek. After parking and getting our gear out, John told us he was going to fish downstream from the bridge to the little country church about a mile away. He liked fishing by himself so us younger angler's would not be any determent in his fishing. Eugene was stuck with Doug and I, we headed upstream.

The water in Little Tumbling was so clear that in a pool of about five feet, the bottom could be viewed clearly as if it was one foot deep. Of course in the eddies, the glare of moving water obscured whatever might be there. Eugene was a good fisherman and not to brag, but Doug and I were not too shabby for boys. We had caught a number of fish in the past few years. John would just say, "We were lucky."

This particular day was a hot day but the trees that shaded both sides of the mountain stream kept us cool. The only drawback to hot weather is that it slows the feeding trout to a standstill. Trout love cold water and thrive on feeding frenzies of flies and hatchlings around the creek. We fished our way up the Little Tumbling for about four hours and none of us had a trout to show for it. We had all three had a hit or two but caught none. We started back toward the Chevy, hitting a hole or two as we worked our way down stream. We talked some and speculated some as to how many fish John caught. Doug and I figured the old pro had to have a couple even on this slow day. Eugene said, "I doubt that John has a fish, considering the action we had."

The shadows were getting pretty long by the time we got back to the car. John was still somewhere down the creek fishing his heart out. Eugene and Doug found themselves a good seat for the wait. I walked over on the bridge and looked deeply into the shadowy waters on the upstream side then on the downstream side. I did not see a fish, but I noticed a big root on the left bank that strutted out into a pool of slow moving water. I thought that to be a prime spot, for mister trout to hide out. I made my way across the little country bridge and down on to the bank where the root stuck out over the water. I approached slowly and went close to the water, hiding myself from the water with the big tree.
I slowly stuck my head around the tree and peered into the pool just behind the great root. What I saw made my heart stop, and then flutter like a butterfly. I saw a big trout rise up near the top of the water to investigate something floating by. I backed off into the cover behind the tree so as not to alarm my unsuspecting quarry. I

Colonel Charles Dahnmon Whitt

thought for a minute as to what kind of bait I should present to this big boy. I couldn't decide if salmon eggs or a night crawler would be best. I decided to put on both, a whole worm with only about I inch threaded on the number four hook, and then I strung on three salmon eggs. I looked the bait over and surmised that the big trout would like the looks of my presentation.

I moved toward the pool from behind the tree, and my dangling crawler latched on to a tall weed. I patiently got it un-hung and got myself into the best position to drop the bait. I slowly dipped the worm and eggs into the most favorable spot to attract the big boy. I moved the end of the pole back and forth while I patiently waited. I didn't wait too long. I saw the shadowy figure that reminded me of a submarine rising for the bait. Now don't jerk too quickly I thought. He had it and my line drew tight, I gave it a yank spontaneously and he was hooked. He kept trying to head under the roots of the tree, but I kept him out of that trap. I worked him up stream and flipped him out on the bank where I fell on him like a bird on a June bug. By now I knew you had to get a finger through a gill to hold a slippery trout. I got him pinned down and my right finger next to my thumb on my right hand through the mouth and gill. He had little teeth chewing on me as I gathered my stringer and

Recollections of Raven & Richlands

strung him onto it. I was sure I had him on the stringer before I yelled at Doug. He was big and thick for a trout, I figured him to be two feet long, but to a kid fisherman, everything appears bigger. At any rate he was a nice one.

I proudly carried him back across the bridge where Doug and even Eugene hurried to meet me. Their eyes were big as they viewed my beauty.

Eugene said, "Nice fish, they will hit anything at about dark."

I didn't answer because I didn't feel like I took unfair advantage of him by the dimming light.

John comes up the bank at about that time and he had one little trout in his creel. He took one look at my fish and asked how I caught it. All the way home we talked about my fish and how I caught it.

"I never heard of anybody fishing with a whole night crawler and three salmon eggs at one time," John went on.

"Me neither, but it works I reckon," I answered.

"Well you got the fish to prove it," said John.

Colonel Charles Dahnmon Whitt

When we got home I thanked John for the fishing trip gave him two dollars for gas, and ran into the house to show off my fish to Dad. He and Mommy were excited to see my big trout.

"Reckon how big it is?" I asked.

"You all never measured it?" Dad asked.

"No, we didn't have anything to measure with," I answered.

Dad laid it out on the counter and took a tape measure from the tip of the tail to the end at the mouth. Now remember things look bigger to kids. It was a real nice fish but not a giant. As trout go around the streams of Virginia it was big. Are you ready?
It measured fifteen inches. I was a little disappointed, but Dad said, "That is a big trout son."

I was so proud of my fish, I hated to clean it and shorten it by cutting off its head. Dad was always so smart about such things; he came up with a good plan that would allow me to show off the fish for some time to come. He took a sharp knife and slit its belly and gently removed its guts, and left the head on for now. He wrapped it up in aluminum foil and placed it into the family freezer. Now any one that came by, I could run and get my trout out and tell the fish story.

The agreement that Dad held me too, about going to church was really the best. I didn't know it at the time, but since I look back and realize what I learned about my Jesus Christ is worth it all. As I said Dad was a smart man, he was also very wise and wanted to show me the truth and way to everlasting life.

I am also thankful for John Lawson, he always allowed me on his many fishing trips. If you have a boy there are two things you should teach him, fishing and going to church.

Chapter 8
Camping On The Lake

I was very young, about six I reckon! I think the year was 1952. Larry my big brother got me to go to the garden with him. Jerry was going about getting other things ready. Daddy would be getting home from a hard day at the mine on a Friday evening and all was set for the four of us to have a three day camp on Holston Lake.

Larry was 5 years older than me and Jerry was two years older than Larry. At any rate I was ready to fish, as was my brothers. A lot of thought had gone into this trip, but I was just a little follower. Dad had agreed to take us on this great adventure and had told Jerry and Larry what to do while he was at work that day.

I was with Dad and my brothers a day or two before when Dad drove all three of us to a friend's home in Doran, a couple of miles from our Raven Virginia home on Mill Creek. Jerry or Larry had found out that a friend Billy had a tent that he would loan us for the outing. Now we had the tent with only half the pegs but we could make the rest out of sticks.

We were in the garden digging potatoes to eat on the trip. It must have been in late summer because potatoes were ready to dig. I can't remember all the details, but I guess Larry was graveling to get out the young spuds without hurting the vines. My job was to pick them up and put them in a box or poke.

I did think it odd that we would be taking potatoes to eat on a camping trip, but I had not given it much thought as to what you are supposed to eat while camping. Hotdogs were always my first choice back then. I do remember that we ate lots of potatoes on that trip; we even ate them for breakfast. Now days that is not a rare thing to have home fries for breakfast, but we had camp fries.

Dad had bought new fishing line and reed poles for Jerry and Larry. I still had my little green sapling with black fishing line that Dad had attached for me. The new fishing line that Dad, Jerry, and Larry were to use was almost white. This was before monofilament was used by fishermen. Only the rich or really dedicated anglers had rods and reels back in the early fifties. At any rate I was rigged differently than Dad and my older brothers with my black fishing line.

Colonel Charles Dahnmon Whitt

Dad got home from work that Friday and headed right into the bathroom to wash off a day's work of coal dirt. If Dad ever came home clean, we all knew at first glance, Dad had not been in the mine. I do remember a few times that Dad would come home early carrying his round miner's dinner bucket. When this happened I knew that Dad had not eaten his lunch, so I would run and greet him to get a sandwich or moon pie. Now that was a real fun thing, even if I was not hungry. This day he had completed his shift and was anxious to get cleaned up, so he could get all packed up and take his three sons over to Holston Lake.

The Tennessee Valley Authority had built a dam on the South Holston River and completed it in 1950. The work on the dam had been started in 1942, but during the war it was put aside for more important work. The work was resumed soon after WW II. The dam was 27 miles south of the Virginia-Tennessee line. This lake was still pretty new, and backed up several miles into Virginia. The fish had been stocked and were getting to be catching size. Of course the Holston River still had whatever fish it had, when it was dammed. News of great catches had abounded, and Dad was going to take us there.

Recollections of Raven & Richlands

After Dad had his bath, Jerry and Larry had most of the stuff loaded up in Dad's 1950 Mercury! It was a neat car, only about two years old. It was a two door and painted black. It is the same car that Jerry got pulled over in, when Dad let him drive without a license, but that is another story.

We had the borrowed tent, old quilts, and blankets, cardboard boxes with produce from the garden, eggs, bread and whatever we had. Back then people didn't run to the store and buy everything for a trip like this. You ate whatever you had.

We motored over to the lake and arrived there in time to find a camp site and set up the tent. It was on a slope like an old road or maybe a planned boat ramp. Dad backed the 1950 Mercury down the hill to about twenty yards from the lake. This left plenty of room between the car and the water for our camp. The ground had been cleared, but there were stumps and rocks everywhere.

Jerry and Larry set up the tent, and the home made pegs worked just as well as the ones that came with the tent. They cleaned out most of the rough rocks and sticks where the tent was set up. I was mostly an observer, but my older brothers often called me lazy. I was watching and learning, I reckon. We got everything ready for the first night, lit a fire and Dad fried some potatoes. Not sure if we got any fishing in that evening or not, but I am sure we looked over the situation.

As darkness fell up on the little camp I was a little scared. We sat around the camp fire and talked for a while before going to bed. I am sure that Dad was tired, he had been up since 5:00 AM, and worked all day in the coal mine before starting out with three boys.

We crawled back inside the little tent and wiggled out a place to sleep. After yakking for a while we fell into slumber. It did not take too long to stay all night on Holston Lake. The Sun was getting up before I wanted to. Brother Jerry was digging under his blankets in search of something. Dad asked him what he was looking for.

"I slept on a rock or something and my back is killing me," Jerry answered.

Larry and I thought it was funny, but Dad told us it would not be funny if we were the ones sleeping on a rock.

After a breakfast of fried eggs and potatoes, we were

ready for a big day of fishing. We were all anxious to try our luck angling. I was the one with the luck on this trip. It seemed every place we went on the big lake I caught a fish. Jerry and Larry took turns baiting my hook and taking fish off for me. They were happy to do it at first, but soon tired of the chore. I was cutting into their fishing time. They caught some fish, but even Dad was not having the luck I enjoyed.

Dad took us up to the end of the cove where the lake ended, and down the other side a little way to some stumps. Dad sat me down on a nice stump and we started fishing. Right off, the magic happened again. There was a school of young carp, I guess about a foot long each. They came to my bait like it was a magnet. I started yanking them out as fast as Jerry and Larry could take them off and re-bait my hook. They begin to complain profusely.

"I can't even get my line in the water because of Dahnmon," said Larry.

"Me neither," Jerry added.

I caught a nice mess of fish, and Dad, Jerry, and Larry caught only a few. I thought it was really fun.

Colonel Charles Dahnmon Whitt

Later in the day Dad was talking to us about my great luck. He had thought it all out about why his little six year old son was catching all the fish. He reasoned that it had to be the fishing line. Remember that Dad, Jerry, and Larry all had new reed poles and white fishing lines. I had the little green sapling, but my fishing line was black. Near the end of our trip, Dad went and bought new line for the three of them. I think it was just fate, that I would be so lucky on my first overnight fishing trip. We ate the fish, even for breakfast.
That was a great trip for a man and his sons to bond and enjoy the great outdoors. I was only six, but so much of the details lodged into my memory bank. Jerry and Larry really had a good time too, but they would have liked it better if I shared more of the fish catching with them.

Dad was around thirty six at the time. This was an unusual trip, because Dad lived through the depression and would not miss a shift. As best I can remember we stayed three nights. It may have been on the week of the coal miner's vacation. Back then the mines would all shut down for a week each summer to allow them a vacation.

That time at the stump, I remember the fish to be Carp,

Larry remembers them to be Bluegills, and Jerry remembers them to be Crappy. It is my story so I'm sticking with Carp.

Dad and my brothers helped me form some fond memories on that special trip. The next Summer I would be stricken with Meningitis and was almost taken to Heaven. God has been so good to me and I have enjoyed my life, especially fishing and hotdogs.

Colonel Charles Dahnmon Whitt

Chapter 9
What Is A Creek?

What is a creek? It was Heaven sent! It is a joy to see and refreshing for a boy to play in!

A creek is like a river but God made it small! It was just right for a boy like me!

My Mommy said stay away from there, you will get hurt, but it drew me like a magnet!

The creek had minnows, those delightful little fish! It had crawdads that looked like little lobsters!

It had big tree roots that stuck out into the water; watch out here for the scary wiggling snake!

It had tall weeds that grew along its banks, Oh! What a delightful place!

I learned so much about life while just playing along the creek!

Recollections of Raven & Richlands

It had ducks, and under its banks it had muskrats too!

I caught my first fish, even though it was small, it meant so much to a boy like me!

It did have some traps I soon learned about; the three leafed Poison Ivy was waiting for me!

When I think of my life and all that I have been through, it was that little creek that prepared me so well! It had training, and comfort too!

I fell through its ice and was really cold! I found that the world was much like this too, if you skate on thin ice you will fall in!

It was refreshing in summer to splash and play, I have never found anything better in this world!

God made my creek, it was just right for a boy like me!

Chapter 10
The BB Gun

For my twelfth birthday, Mom gave me a Daisy Defender BB Gun, with certain stipulations. I had to agree not to shoot at any birds. I agreed spontaneously so I could get my hands on the new air rifle. The Daisy Defender was a special model; it had a magazine like the pump models and only held fifty BB's. It was also more powerful than most air rifles.

"Now son, if I ever hear of you shooting birds I will take your BB gun, and you will never get it back," Mommy told me.

"I promise, I won't shoot birds," I answered quickly.

"Here is your birthday present, please be careful with it," Mommy said as she handed me the most precious gift a boy could get.

I took the new air rifle everywhere I went during the next few days, and did not even think of shooting at any live targets. As time went on I became quite proficient with the great little rifle. All the boys were envious of my treasure. I could shoot farther and more accurate than any of my friends.

After several months passed the temptation grew, and I yielded. My neighbors, the Kennedy's, saved scraps of food for their hogs. They had a bucket hanging at the end of their clothes line. We called it a slop bucket back then. The bucket was up out of reach of dogs, cats, and other critters that may want to feed upon the enticing morsels. The bucket did attract a long line of black birds that lined up on the clothes line. This was my temptation, and one day I could not resist.

I had to be stealth, not to get a shot at the birds, but not to get caught. This day only one black bird set on the line close to the slop bucket. I looked at my house, my grandmother's house and roundabout for any witness that may report an unauthorized shooting. The coast was clear so I took the opportunity to try my air rifle on a living, breathing bird.

I gave one more, quick look around, raised the rifle and aimed at the feathered target. I squeezed the trigger and the deadly missile was on the way. What happened next was unbelievable; I hit the black bird in the head and killed it instantly. It didn't fall to the ground; it had a death grip on the clothes line and just hung there

Colonel Charles Dahnmon Whitt

upside down, as evidence of my mischief. The bird kept swinging back and forward to torment me.

I panicked, I had to get that bird to turn loose of the clothes line and hide the evidence. I laid down my prized weapon and ran in a bolt toward the swinging bird. I jumped up and hit the bird with my hand to knock it down, and this only caused it to swing round and round.

Oh my, this bird was determined to wreak revenge on its slayer. What was I going to do? I jumped with all my might with both hands extended and caught the bird with a death grip. With all my weight and might I yanked the bird free of the clothes line. I threw the dead thing over in the weeds to hide the evidence. I looked all around and as far as I could tell, no one saw this crime but Almighty God.

I was instantly sorry for my actions, it was the first thing I ever killed, and I was sorry about that. I was also sorry for breaking my promise to Mommy. My crime was hidden; I would just have to live with it.
Almost fifty years later when Mommy was in poor health and not too long for this world, I confessed the whole thing to her. She smiled and said you have been

punished enough by keeping this secret for all of these years. I knew I was forgiven, and felt relieved for killing the swinging black bird. I can still see that bird hanging upside down and swinging back and forth, in my mind.

Mom Edith, not long after Dad had put the siding on the old house. Notice there is still no paint.

Colonel Charles Dahnmon Whitt

Chapter 11
Raising Rabbits In Raven

I was around ten years old when Dad let me purchase a pet rabbit from the Joyce boys. They were our neighbors not too far away. The Joyce boys were my friends and enemies, according to what day it was. But that is another story. Now back to the Bunny Tale.

I got chicken wire and built a pen, and also a cage up off the ground with hardware cloth in the bottom. This was in there so when my rabbit did his business the little pellets fell out on the ground. I learned that from the Joyce boys.

As time went by, my Pete grew up and he was a girl rabbit, to my surprise. The Joyce boys told me I should bring her out for a visit and let her get bred, that way I could have little baby bunnies for sale. The idea sounded pretty good to me, so I took her courting out at the Joyce boys' house. I did not bother to ask Dad, I just knew he would like the idea. If I sold the new babies I could give him some money for feed and pen making stuff. I found out, rabbits get their babies real quick, about three weeks. Somehow I got it in my head that mommy rabbits always have babies in increments of seven. I don't remember how I learned this important thing, dreamed it or maybe the Joyce boys.

I told Dad that I took Pete courting, and he was not as pleased about it as I was. I told him that Pete would have seven babies before long. "Now you don't know she will have seven babies!" Dad said.
"When did you take her out there?" he asked.

"About two weeks ago I reckon, and yes she will get seven babies," I said insistently.

Dad just shook his head and smiled as if to say, "Wait and see."
Now you have to picture this, Dad bought all the fencing, boards, and nails, not to mention food for my rabbit. Now she was going to be a mommy rabbit.

The short gestation period for rabbits is only three weeks and it passed quickly. I went out one morning and Pete had dug a hole under a board in the floor of the pen. She had pulled all the fur off her chest and had lost substantial weight. I investigated the situation and was pleased to be the owner of seven new bunny babies. I couldn't wait for Dad to get home from work to tell him the good news. I also wanted him to know that mommy rabbits do always have seven babies the first time.

When Dad got home that evening in his normal coal dirty clothes and black face, I ran to greet him and tell about Pete having babies.(Dad was a coal miner)

"Dad, Pete had seven babies just like I told you," I said proudly.

"She did, now that is just a coincidence that she had seven," Dad replied.

After Dad had his bath and ate supper, Mom and Dad went out to see Pete's babies.

"They sure are cute little things," Mommy said.
I agreed and reemphasized that she had seven just like I said.

Even Mommy agreed with Daddy, rabbits don't always have seven babies the first time. Didn't Pete just prove that they do, I thought. Time went on and the babies grew up quickly. The Joyce boys suggested I bring Pete courting again. It sounded like a splendid idea; I could picture the fourteen new bunny babies in my young mind.

Dad had not complained about buying rabbit food for the now eight rabbits I had. After I took Pete courting again I told Dad about the new development and that Pete was expecting fourteen new baby bunnies. Dad did not share the excitement and anticipation that I did. Now Dad disagreed with me again about how many babies mommy rabbits have.

Sometimes Mommies and Daddies seem so dumb, I thought.

Daddy implied he would not be too happy with all the new little mouths to feed. Fourteen I knew.

In no time at all Pete got fat and pulled the fur off her chest again. I went out one morning to find Pete had babies again. I pulled out all the new little arrivals and counted each one. Guess what, she had fourteen new bunny babies. As before I could hardly wait to tell Daddy when he got home from the mine. As soon as he got home I ran to tell him of the grand news.
"Pete had babies last night," I told with much pride.
"How many did she have?" Daddy asked as if to prove a point.

"Fourteen," I said proudly.

"Don't you know that mommy rabbits always have fourteen babies the second time?" I asked as a pro rabbit breeder. "That is just a coincidence," Daddy insisted.

Now Pete had proved that mommy rabbits always have fourteen the second time, not to mention that she proved they have seven the first time. After a couple of weeks passed I mentioned that Pete would have twenty one babies next time.

"Oh No, she will not, you are not taking Pete courting anymore," Dad said in no uncertain terms I now had twenty two rabbits, guess what; Dad wanted me to trade off some of my baby bunnies. I guess me and Pete finally convinced Daddy that mommy rabbits have babies in increments of seven!

Chapter 12
Nails and Boards

At an early age I found that I loved tools and making things! I guess this is what led to my vocation as a Sheet Metal Worker. Dad noticed that I had interest in hand tools and he (Santa) encouraged me by giving me a little tool set one Christmas. It was not a toy tool set, but a functional set on a smaller scale. The hammer was small as well as the hand saw. They were real tools that Dad would borrow when he wanted to do a little job. He would just grab out a tool, rather than going out to the smoke house to get his! I was pleased that Dad would use my tools; this made me know that they were real McCoy's! Of course I used Dads hammer and saws; I think that was one reason that Santa brought me my own tools that Christmas.

I became quiet proficient at driving nails, a friend Kenny and I would build tree houses and other club houses! We would go up and down Mill Creek and salvage the boards that high water would bring us! God had put some tall ash trees on the upper end of my empire. (Dad's Lot) Kenny and I would nail boards of about two feet long up the trees to create a ladder. We would get way up in the tree to the first big forks and build our fort there. Kenny was a little older and bigger than me, so

Colonel Charles Dahnmon Whitt

he would pull up the boards I tied on the rope. It is a wonder we are here today! We never fell, but a board came untied as Kenny was pulling it up one day. The board was light because it was rotten. It fell across my head and broke.

As I staggered around, Kenny yelled down at me!

"You all right?" he asked.
I whimpered out a little whine.

Kenny saw that I was alright, and said, "Damn, your head is harder than that board!"

I didn't see the humor in it!

One of my projects was a new club house built on the ground. It was in a flood plain so I built it on stilts! I knew when the spring rains came Mill Creek would back up from the flooded Clinch River.

I was really pleased with my accomplishment, until my big brother saw it.

He laughing said, "It looks like a toilet!"

Recollections of Raven & Richlands

Another project I had was to convert my 4 Radio Flyer wagon wheels into a wooden downhill racer! I used my imagination and added a steering wheel and hand brake! It was a fun thing to fly down the old gravel road on church house hill, pretending I was in a great race!

As I said, I got good at driving nails, and I used up Dad's nails about as fast as he would buy them. I can still hear him fussing when he would look for a nail to repair something!

"That young-un gets every nail I bring in," Dad would say.

Yet I don't think he minded too much. He never ever said leave my stuff alone. He kept his tools and nails out in an oak board building that was once used as a smoke house. Those boards were as hard as steel!
I went to the Richlands Fair one year, and saw a way to get a Teddy Bear at one of the gambling joints. They had a 4 X 4 set up like a saw horse. They started 3 two inch nails in the board. You would put up a Quarter (25 cents) and try to drive all the nails into the board with three hits of the hammer. I noticed that they started the nails on an angle to make you bend the nails while striking them.

Colonel Charles Dahnmon Whitt

I plopped down my quarter and took the hammer. I aimed the hammer on the exact angle and gave each nail a strong blow. Bam, Bam, Bam, the nails all three were driven down to the head in the 4 X 4.

The woman gave me a big Teddy Bear! Her boss hurried over to her, and started instructing her as to how to start the nails.

"I did start them on an angle," she said, "That kid can drive nails!"

I walked away with my trophy, knowing I could have cleaned them out of Teddy Bears!

Chapter 13
Fun In Raven & Richlands

While growing up in the Stinson Bottom section of Raven, VA; I had several playmates through the years. Some of them were older and some were younger than I. Some have become lifelong friends.

We had a favorite field we played in, it was a vacant lot. It was at the bottom of a steep hill and on top of the hill was our favorite place to sit and plot. It was a wonderful place to sit and talk, we had big rocks made just for us it seemed. We sat upon the rocks under the shade of mighty oak trees. We kids spent many hours on the rocks talking and many hours playing in the field.

Girls and boys both played on the field, but it was mostly us boys. We met there most every day. There were the Adkins kids, but they moved away when I was young, the Johnson kids moved in after them. There was the older Cordle girls that got too big to play after a while, later there were the younger kids of the Cordles, Dennis, Randall, and Doug.

The Kennedy boys, the Farmer kids and the Hodge kids were there part of the time. The Shelton, Joyce,

Colonel Charles Dahnmon Whitt

Kennedy and Cordle kids were the regulars along with me and my brothers, the Whitts. We all played together and like kids do, we loved each other and at times we hated each other. We always got over our mad spells pretty quick.

We kids played basketball, with the goal provided by the Cordle family. We played some rough football games and we played baseball games. Our baseball games were somewhat different than the organized version. We played with a rubber ball and instead of tagging out the runner we threw the ball at them. Usually we threw it pretty hard, but being rubber it had little pain. I remember we whooped and hollered to our hearts content. Boy those were fun days.

We played all the old school games also, like Red Rover come over, rope jumping and marble playing. If we got bored we simply invented new games. The steep hill by our field was covered with broom sage. We found out that if you got a big piece of card board, it offered us a grand ride down the hill. It was like a magic carpet ride; we would do that for hours.

Recollections of Raven & Richlands

Now as seasons changed we changed with them. In winter instead of cardboard, we brought out our Radio Flyer sleighs and rode down the hill on the snow.

Speaking of sleigh riding we often took our sleds up on Elswick's hill, now that was a ride, a fast and long ride. You had to be careful at the bottom or you would go in the creek. If the creek was frozen over we simply rode right on through.

Sometimes the Stinson Bottom kids would take their sleighs up to the old white church and join the West Raven kids to ride down the long hill. (Route 67 from Raven to Honaker)

Now that could be dangerous as cars would try to navigate the slick hill between us riding our sleighs. One thing we loved to do was to make long trains of sleigh riders. This was done by lying on your sleigh and putting your feet in the front of the sleigh following you. Sometimes we would have a dozen of us brave souls in the train. The person in front would do the driving and he would take us on a zigzag run. We looked much like a giant snake meandering down the road.

Of course we always had a bon fire to warm by, some kid would donate an old car tire to burn and the smoke got really bad.

Now in the spring, the windy season brought out the kite flyers. Some of our kites were homemade, but most could be bought for around a quarter. We had many kites, some with long tails of torn cloth and some even had the box kites. I never could figure out how the box kites flew, but they did. There were very stable and loved to ride the high currents from a lofty place like the McGlothin Hill. The box kite could even get boring after a while; it never dived or did much dancing in the wind like the regular kites did.

We Raven kids never got bored too much; we always found something to entertain us. We had no video games or cell phones. In the deep cold days of winter we played things like checkers and dominos.

Television was a new thing in the 1950's, if you could get one good channel down in the mountains you were flying. There are many stories about running the TV wire called "Jacob's Ladder," up on the lofty hills to get a better picture. It turned out for us that we got it just as good down in Stinson Bottom. We got one good channel.

Not only did we play together, most of us were fisher kids and hunter kids. We all had BB guns, later we had archery sets, at least a bow and a few arrows. We became quite proficient with them. As we got older we had 22's and shotguns to hunt with.

I think I could write a giant book just on our ability to find things to do. Have you ever heard of a Carbide cannon? You got a baking powder can and punched a little hole near the bottom. Next you dropped in one piece of carbide that was ready available at the Raven Super Market. You spit on the carbide, put the lid on the baking powder can. Got a long stick and put a match on it. You would cautiously stick the little flame to the hole on the can. Boom, that lid would fly high in the sky.

One great source of entertainment was going to the show, at the Raven Show House, (Raven Theater). Now we didn't know any difference, but we thought cowboy movies were the only ones made. The Show House was kinda sophisticated; they played Guy Lombardo music before starting the cartoons and movie.

Colonel Charles Dahnmon Whitt

It seemed all the cowboy shows were pretty much alike, some poor woman would be in danger of losing her ranch to the crooks, and a brave cowboy would come and save the day. We thought the worst movies were the ones that the cowboy would kiss the lady then ride off into the sunset. We didn't go for that kissing stuff.

Now the Wilson family owned the Raven Theater and the ice cream parlor. They had the best ice cream and hotdogs in Virginia.

The really good part was the cost of these fine things, it cost 12 cents to get in, the hotdogs were a dime and that was with sauce and all. You could get your comic book there for a nickel, now those books would be worth hundreds of dollars if you kept them in great shape. Mostly the comic books were worn out because we always traded them for others after we read them.

The Raven Theater was one of the prominent spot in Raven. I do remember one odd thing. They never had any restroom facilities. After us boys sit through a cowboy movie and drink a large cherry-smash we were ready to. There was a long wooden garage across the road next to coal creek. As soon as the movie was over, we boys ran across the street to pee behind it. I never thought about it until I began to write this book, but where did the girls go? They must have had to wait until they got home! Of course as a boy I always thought girls were a little strange anyway.

A lot of old Raven is still standing today, but neglect and blight has taken a toll on the once nice little town. Now there is a group of native Raven folk working on restoring the Raven Theater and ice cream parlor and making it into a coal miner's museum. I am all for that. If they are successful in making a fine museum out of the Old Show House it will instill the pride back into Raven. Who knows many of the old building may come under restoration plans also. I hope so. The old Show House has made many memories for all the folks in and around Raven.

I have many memories of Raven, but jumped into my head while writing today. I remember when they poured the sidewalks in Raven. They added something red on top of the newly poured cement. I guess it was to make it cure out faster. The red stuff went away in time and the old sidewalks are gray and worn today.

Raven was a place of freedom and fun in those days; a kid could walk to and from the show or visit friends and

Colonel Charles Dahnmon Whitt

never be in any danger. Even going by Cap Justice's beer joint was not a problem.

Back in those days all the parents watched out for all the children. Some parents would even spank a neighbor child if he or she needed it. Wow what would they say today?

I remember one such case; I was being tended to by my neighbor Goldie Shelton while Mommy went somewhere. Now Goldie's, daughter Bertina and I were about the same age. We were left to play on the family front porch. I don't know whose idea it was but we decided it would be fun to dig the dirt out of Goldie's flowers. That brought quick judgment and correction. We both got our hinnies spanked and learned a good lesson that day. Today that would be unheard of!

When Mommy got back, Goldie told her side of the story, I don't think I ever got to tell mine. Mommy didn't like it too much but she was close friends with Goldie and knew I probably deserved a smack on the hind end. My mother had even delivered Goldie's son Philbert when he came into this world.

Oh, I wish it was like it was back in the early days of Raven. We all knew how we stood and were loved. Neighbors were neighbors and were always ready to extend a hand to those in need.

"We thought we were rich! As it turns out we were, in discipline, God, and Country standards!"

Raven and Richlands was a wonderful place to grow up. Many folks that grew up there have become model citizens and professional educated people, many like me served our country in time of war.

Colonel Charles Dahnmon Whitt

Land Mark on Little River. Famous for Hams Hanging outside. Wardell Hams!

Recollections of Raven & Richlands

The old building still stands.

Coal Miners Memorial in Richlands, Virginia.

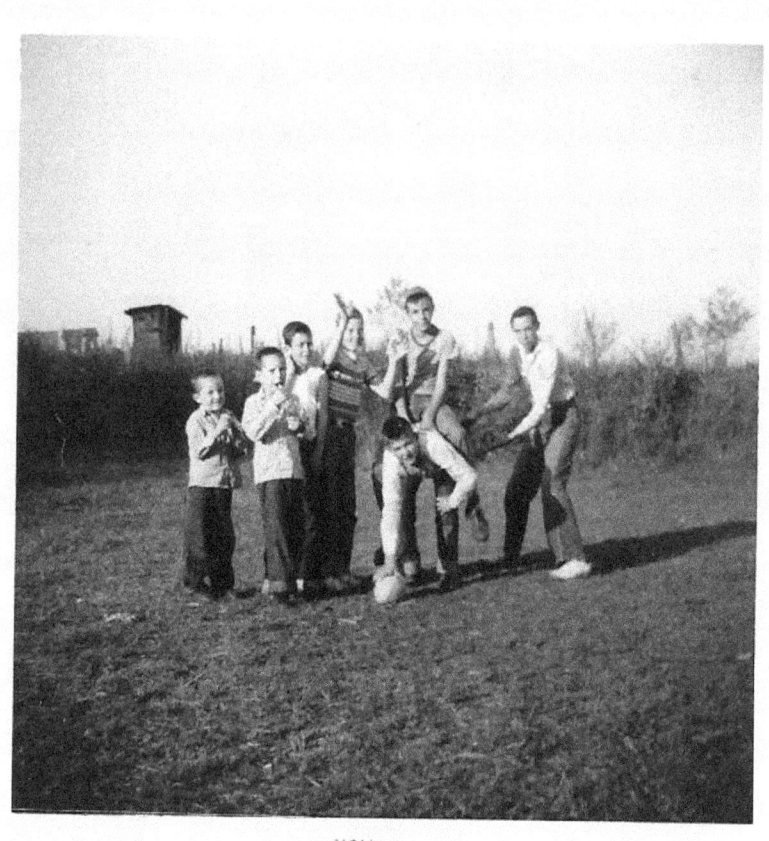

"Stinson Bottom Gang" L to R; Randall, Dennis, Philbert, Doug, Billy on my back, Carl and I am the center over the ball.

MY Show House, the Raven Theater, in Raven, VA

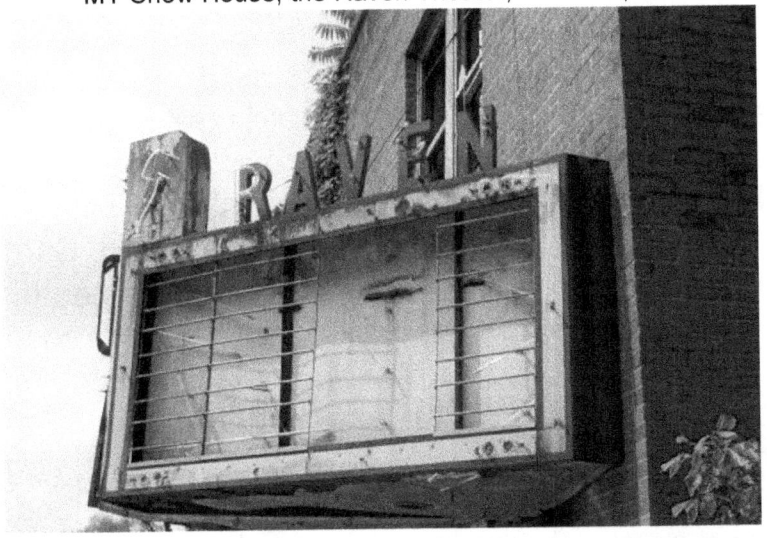

It is now being restored to a coal museum and ice-cream parlor.

Chapter 14
Aunt Mary Ball Pack & Pappy

A tribute to Raven and Richlands would not be complete without remembering Mary Ball Pack and Pappy.

I think my earliest memories of Mrs. Pack and Pappy were in the late nineteen forties. The Packs had a store on the right side of the road on Raven Hill, Route 67. They sold feed and convenient items such as bread, some produce, milk and bake goods. In seasons they would carry whatever the folks wanted like canning jars and lids and seed and much more.

It was Christmas time and we heard that Santa Claus always stopped at the Pack's store so Dad and Mom loaded us up and took us to see the old elf. There he was, the jolly old Saint Nick all dressed in red. Santa made it a point to show us the soot that adorned his sleeve. He said he just couldn't keep his nice red suit clean as he went up and down the many chimneys in his travels. I was in awe of being in the presence of such a majestic being as Santa Clause. I must confess I was a little scared of the old elf. To me it was kinda like meeting an angel or something like that.

Colonel Charles Dahnmon Whitt

After I grow up a few years more I figured it out. Old Santa was none other than Pappy Pack.

Our family was really close to the Packs as they were good people and good friends. Mrs. Pack was a Christian, not sure about Pappy, but we are not supposed to judge. As far as I know he is sitting around the old potbellied stove in Heaven.

I am not sure what year it was but the Packs bought property across the road on the left as you go up Raven Hill. There they built a nice concrete block building with two stories and on up the hill they built two dwelling houses. They moved their store to the new building and moved into the new house nearest to the store.

The new store was equipped with a large pot-belled stove for heat. This is where you could usually find Pappy Pack, sitting around the stove and spitting tobacco juice in the ash pan. If he missed it would hit the hot stove and make a hissing sound and the aroma was kinda nice to smell. He always had seats to accommodate friends that may stop by. Also he kept a small table all set up with a checker board and he dearly loved to play checkers. Pappy knew about relaxing and Mrs. Mary Ball Pack was real industrious and the money maker in the marriage.

The new store was much larger and had room for 100 pound sack of hog chop and other animal feeds. Mrs. Pack kept a good stock of canning supplies in the summer and fall and kept a good supply of seed and onion sets, even plants like tomato, cabbage, and pepper plants for folk's gardens. With all of this going on, the store had an unforgettable aroma. It was just a nice relaxing smell that made you want to stay awhile.

Mrs. Pack also dealt in flower arrangements and even oil paintings and of course everyday grocery items.

Both of my brothers worked there part time but not at the same time. Jerry worked for the Packs for a year or so and then Larry worked for them. I am sure it was a good experience and also a learning experience for both of them. I think you could get a wonderful education while working in this little country store and your boss would have been just great to work for.

I remember one summer day Larry was watching the store and I was with him, guess he was watching me also. The bread man came to stock the bread and bakery items. Larry knew the man and asked if he had any free samples. The nice bread man gave us both a

Honey Bun. Man, they tasted so good, guess we were hungry or maybe it was just that we got them free. Mrs. Pack was very dignified even though she did not mind getting her hands dirty. She, being a Ball by birth claimed to be kin to Martha Ball Washington the first "First Lady" of our country. I do not doubt that she was.

Mrs. Pack was very artistic and loved working with flowers, oil painting and other artistic ventures. She made arrangements to meet the needs of the local folks for Decoration Day, (Memorial Day) and for funerals, really for whatever anyone wanted flowers for.

Mrs. Pack loved to express herself with oil paint and brush on canvas and she did many paintings as she kept a canvas on an easel most of the time. Her paintings were always bright and cheerful which matched her aged eyes and disposition.

Mrs. Pack loved the local kids and wanted to share her love of art with us all. She set up a little art class for us on Saturday mornings and helped us get little painting kits and a canvas. She charged us; I think fifty cents a lesson. She even bought cheap framed prints and saved the frames for us. I am not sure how many kids went to these classes but remember Bertina Shelton and Phyllis Reedy took the class along with me.

Mrs. Pack taught us the basics of oil painting as we worked on our own little master piece. Mrs. Pack encouraged us and I remember she said I was a bold painter as I liked the bigger brush and much paint. I still have my first painting; it was pretty good for a kid, but not a master piece.

Other ways she encouraged me was to buy some of my other art. I picked up little piece of asbestos board that dad had lying around. Yes I said asbestos; we did not know the danger of that stuff. I then went to the Clinch River below the swinging bridge where folks forded the river in normal pool. There on the sand beach I picked up big muscle shells and let them dry out. Then I took them home and glued them to the asbestos and let the beautiful mother of pearl show forth. Mrs. Pack bought these from me and set them up to sell. I didn't get much and I am not sure if she sold any, but it was a wonderful encouragement to a boy.

Mrs. Pack loved going to the white church, Raven Methodist Church, and was very active in it.

Pappy loved to tell stories and was not known for hard work, but he may have been a hard worker back in his younger days. He kinda depended on Mrs. Mary to take care of things.

One story I still remember was how he killed seven turkeys with one shot. When Pappy was young living in Smyth County Virginia the turkeys were thick in the woods so Pappy thought out a good trick to get several turkeys with only one shot as powder and lead was hard to come by. He went out in the woods to find a knoll where the turkeys had been gathering to scratch for food. He baited the knoll with cracked corn and waited a couple of days and went back. The turkeys had been there and all the corn was gone. Pappy found a bush that would make a good blind, walked straight from the bush and made a furrow to line up with the bush. Then he gently sprinkled in cracked corn as if planting it but did not cover it up. Next morning before the sun came up Pappy was behind the bush all lined up with and looking straight through the furrow. He heard the turkeys talking back and forth with their gobble, gobble talk. Finally one came to the furrow and saw the treat. He started eating and others rushed to the furrow. Finally several birds were lined up on both sides sticking their heads down into the furrow and picking the corn. Bang went the old riffle and seven turkeys were jumping round with their heads blown off and the other turkeys scrambled from the unknown danger. It was a bunch of commotion Pappy said. He went over and gathered up the seven turkeys and tied their feet together so he could carry all of them. Pappy had a mess of turkey all taken with one shot. Believe it or not!

Now Pappy loved horses so he bought a nice saddle horse and made arrangements with Mrs. Elswick that had a nice pasture on the hill known as Elswick's Hill, yes the same one we sleighed on in the snow. This hill was above the little Mill Creek Valley above the creek falls.

Jack Young a good friend of mine that has gone on to be with the Lord. Jack Young that was the Police Chief for a number of years, as a boy decided to ride Pappy's horse. He was near the fence so he climbed from the fence to the back of the horse. The horse didn't know Jack Young so he bucked Jack off to the ground. Oh you never saw such a crooked arm on a boy when he was able to get up. It looked like a rainbow without all the pretty colors. Yes, my friend Jack broke that arm. He went home and confessed to his dad and they went on to the hospital and got him a cast. On the way back home Roscoe, Jack's father stopped at the Packs and marched Jack in to see Pappy. Jack had a broken arm

Colonel Charles Dahnmon Whitt

and was already in a time of suffering but he stood up like a man and apologized to Pappy for getting on his horse. This was a lesson well learned by Jack and all of us boys; you don't ride another man's horse.

Now Pappy or Mary Pack never drove nor had a driver's license. They took cabs, buses or had folks take them on trips. I think they ordered things from wholesalers by phone or occasionally had a friend take them. One time I remember, the Packs wanted to travel back to a reunion and see their old home area of Smyth County Virginia, so they asked my Mom and Dad to take them on a Saturday. Dad agreed to drive them and it was a fun trip for me as I got to go also.

We loaded up early on a Saturday morning and headed to Smyth County. It was Dad, Mom, Pappy, Aunt Mary Pack and I had begun calling her. Right off the bat Aunt Mary Pack started watching for churches as we traveled. It was amazing all the little churches that dotted the western Virginia country side.

One of our first stops was a Southern Style mansion that had a spiral stair case. It was plush and richer looking than any house I had ever been in. The Lady of the house flirted with Dad and Mom was not too happy about that. Then we moved on to the reunion on Smith Mountain Lake. There were lots of people there and Pappy and Aunt Mary had a wonderful time reuniting with old friends and I guess kin. Pappy kept talking about them having mutton. Now mutton was a new word to me and I learned that it was sheep meat. Well I got to try some and found it to be good. Some folks shy away from it because they picture the sad faces of the sheep.. It is kinda like some folks don't like venison because of the sad eyes of the deer. I don't know why we never had mutton at our house, guess it was expensive, but there was an abundance of sheep raised in southwest Virginia and still are today. Mostly they are raised for their wool. The trip was a success for the Packs and even Dad and Mom had a good day, especially making the Packs happy.

I grew up around Pappy and Aunt Mary Pack and learned to love them. Aunt Mary was not a beautiful woman, but inside she was a saint. On the other hand Pappy could be ornery at times. By saying this let me tell you what he would say to me as a teenager when I came by to see them; Pappy would ask me how is your Copperostic today? If no ladies were present he would make a measurement with his fingers and ask, about this long? I think he meant my male member, but if ladies were present he did the same but, meant my disposition of sorts. Basically how did I feel that day? Pappy would sit back and laugh, then he would ask me if I would play a game of checkers with him. He was good at playing checkers, he had lots of practice and maybe he cheated some, I just don't know.

The Mary Ball Pack store is still standing today as a reminder of the good old days in Raven. Our neighbor and friend Checker Cordle took over the store for some time and ran it after the Packs gave it up because of their old age.

The one thing about Checker running it was that he decided to collect Two Dollar Bills. The odd currency was plentiful in Tazewell and Russell County during those years and I never knew why. Checker finally quit the collection as he said he just couldn't afford to save so many. The Packs, both Pappy and Aunt Mary Ball Pack were greatly respected in the Raven and Richlands area of ole Virginia.

Recollections of Raven & Richlands

Chapter 15
Pete The Parakeet

Right by the new Packs store was another little business. Facing the Pack's store to the left Jim Ball had a salvage business where he would buy scrap metal of all kinds and I think he would buy dried wild roots like may-apple and Ginseng. I did not remember too much about Jim but I remember one big thing, He came and took away my Pete, my parakeet. Now to give Jim a fair shake I need to tell the whole story.

About a quarter of a mile from Jim Ball's business lived my grandpa, Charles Henry Whitt, right behind the Old White Church. He was out on his porch one day and noticed something different. There was a bright colored little bird that looked like a parrot. The little bird was greenish yellow and was much smaller than a parrot. It was on his porch banister and didn't seem to be afraid. Grandpa gently walked over and caught the little bird and figured it must be a parakeet that got away from somebody. There was no one around that he knew had such a bird.

He thought it would be a good pet for his grandson Dahnmon, (ME). He brought it down and gave it to me. We got a nice cage and some seed and I was tickled to

Colonel Charles Dahnmon Whitt

death with my new birdie. I named him or her, Pete. After several days passed, Pete was right at home and I loved him so much. Somehow some way, Jim Ball heard that I had a little parakeet that Charles Henry Whitt had caught. He and his daughter came to our house and ask Dad if they could see our parakeet and explained that his daughter's little bird escaped and flew off.

Dad, being always honest, fair and friendly let Jim and his daughter come in and the daughter ran straight to the cage where Pete was playing and exclaimed, it's him dad, it is my bird.

Dad knowing that my bird was caught from the porch of grandpa reasoned that most likely my little Pete was indeed their bird. Now according to my thinking, she lost him and he flew to grandpa and without him catching Pete he would still be out flying free. Thinking all of this through I reasoned that Pete was my bird.

Dad said to them that they could take him being it was most likely their escaped bird. I ran and cried as it broke my heart to let my little friend go. Since we had a cage and seed, it was not long before Dad and Mom got me a little blue parakeet.

Recollections of Raven & Richlands

Chapter 16
Go Fly A Kite

As I grew up in the hills of southwest Virginia, I learned many things from my big brothers. One of these was the art of building and flying kites. Every year when March came in, the wind came with it. That brought out the kite flyers. I remember that Jerry and Larry would let out so much line that there kite would appear as a tiny dot dancing in the wind way above the McGlothlin Ridge we flew on. They flew way across the Clinch River bottom.

One evening Jerry was flying his kite way out, when suppertime came. Mommy went out and hollered for him to come and eat. Jerry had a dilemma, how could he wind in his kite and hurry off the ridge and get to the house for supper? When Mommy hollered, you listened and you ran home! Jerry started winding it in and realized that it would take some-time. Back then folks sat down to eat as a family not as come and go like today. Jerry knew he had to cut the line, or come up with a good commonsense answer.

Jerry looked over the situation and saw a lone fence post a few yards away. He simply walked over and tied his kite string to the post and scooted down the ridge to supper. Jerry told everyone at the table that his kite was flying itself with the help of a fence post. This brought some smiles and even a laugh. Someone said that thing would be on the ground before he could do his chores and get back to the kite. I am not sure, but maybe Jerry didn't have to wash dishes that day, but I remember he got back up on the ridge and casually wound in the kite.

Jerry and Larry built their own kites most of the times and repaired them as needed. They would use the paper from the drycleaners. Back then plastic was not in wide use. The light paper, tan in color made good kite material. The only thing it lacked the bright colors of the store bought kites. I also made a few kites as I learned the skill from my older brothers.

Some other things I learned was the way to wind in a kite and to add a tail for high wind usage. My brothers had learned a method to expedite bringing the kite in. They would wind the kite string the normal way until they got a ball started in the middle of their stick. The stick was about an inch in diameter and six to eight inches long. After they got a nice ball in the middle they would wind end over end crossing the ball which brought string in faster. As for tails, they would use light weight rags and tie them at the bottom of the kite to keep it from nose diving. It was experimental as to how much tail you used on a given day according to the amount of wind.

I bought myself a box kite one March. To this day I don't understand how they fly, but they fly nicely. They can become boring after a while just setting up there riding the wind. I have not seen a box kite in many years; someone should put them back on the market.

As I got older I became interested in model airplanes, the ones with the little engines. I got my first one for Christmas. It was plastic and had short lines to fly it with. It was more of a learning experience than anything else.

The way you controlled them was quiet simple. The elevator on the back of the model planes moved up and down just like the real ones. You had a handle with two lines attached. You held the handle vertical as you flew the planes. The lines went into the left wing and into the fuselage to a turn-tee. From there two lines went back to the elevator. As you angle the handle back the elevator raised thus the model plane rose and if you angled the handle down the plane went down. The rudder was fixed in place, turned to the right thus causing the model plane to try and fly away from you and keeping the lines tight.

As I learned about this fun hobby, I moved up to building much larger planes from balsa wood and silk-span. After buying the kit you would assemble the plane by gluing the wood pieces together and cover with the silk-span. Next you would paint the silk-span with model plane dope, a clear substance about the same as clear fingernail polish. As the dope dried the silk-span shrink up to a strong tight skin. Then you could add color paint to your own taste.

The planes according to size would require different size engines. I remember I got my dream engine, a McCoy 35; it would deliver six tenths of horsepower and sounded like a screaming demon. I began to think that anything would fly if you put a McCoy 35 on it.

I had many crashes and learned to repair the planes. This developed into a new design of my own. I built a flying wing and it flew. It was heavy and bulky which made it slower than most of the model planes.

I got pretty good at flying my planes and would have

dog fights with my friends. We would both stand together in the flying circle and have two of our friends start the engines and launch them together. We added about three feet of crepe paper one inch wide to the tails. As we chased each other we would cut off the paper of each other's plane with the spinning propellers.

I got a good background in aviation by building and flying these little planes on 50 feet of thin steel cable. I once was flying as a thunder storm was approaching and the air became filled with static electricity. The charge shot up the little cables and was jolting me pretty good. I wanted to turn loose but I knew my plane would crash. I held on dancing around until the fuel ran out and I landed my plane.

As I stated I got a good background in aviation and when I joined the U.S. Navy I put this information on my application for school and was sent to naval aviation school to be an Aviation Structural Mechanic. A few times while in service I repaired the fabric tears on the old Beech Craft C-45 and C-47 elevators just like I did on the little model planes. The only difference was that you sewed the tear with a baseball stitch and placed a piece of fabric over the tear and put the dope to it.

While serving in the Navy I got to fly often up and down

the east coast from Florida to Rhode Island as an air crewman. My hobbies as a young person paid off as I put it to use in the U.S. Navy.

Chapter 17
The N & W Railroad

Living in Raven, I always will remember the old coal fired steam engines huffing and puffing down the line.

This is the old Raven rail road depot. I walked by it many times going and coming from Raven school.

Colonel Charles Dahnmon Whitt

From my earliest days I remember the whistle blowing from the trains as they rattled down the line. My mom told me that when I was real young and suffered with rheumatic fever that the blowing of the train horns scared me half to death. I don't remember the days I was afraid of the trains, instead I remember loving them. The mystery of the giant fire breathing iron horses still fascinates me today.

I remember the days of old, how I lay in bed at night and listened to the peaceful sounds the trains made as they came into my hearing. I first heard the distant horn of the old steam engine, as it blew at the Raven Crossing, then in a little bit I could hear the rattling and clicking as the train came nearer to my home. It was such a peaceful sound and it made me know I was safe in my bed and had a new world to wake up to every morning in Raven.

I am pretty sure that the Norfolk and Western railroad was the last to retire the old coal fired steam engines.

Now the old Raven depot was a land mark for years. It was still used when I was a kid. I remember coming up on my 13th birthday, Mom told me I could get a bicycle so she took me to the Raven Super Market, a land mark

Recollections of Raven & Richlands

in itself, to look at bicycles. None would suit me as I had a special bike in mind. I had seen an English racing bike with 3 speeds and hand brakes. It was made in England by a company named Armstrong. The racer was actually cheaper than the heavy typical American bikes. I still remember the cost, it was $39.00 dollars delivered right to the Raven N & W depot. I remember going to the depot with dad and picking it up. Wonder why people don't ship on trains anymore?

When the folks that worked the depot wanted to send a signal to a passing train they would put a certain number of torpedoes on the rail. When the big iron wheels ran over them they would make a loud noise. I don't know the code as to how many blast mean what, but I do now the torpedoes were put on the rails with lead strips. We boys would gather this left over strips of lead and use it for fishing sinkers.

Also when the trains stopped at the Raven depot the men would put sand on the rails to help get it started again. It had something to do with getting the big steam engines going. When the train was ready to pull out the engine would receive the steam and the big wheels would spin and then slow as it began to pull the hundreds of tons of coal and iron and other goods. We kids loved to watch the big fire breathing steam squirting iron horse take off. There is nothing like it today.

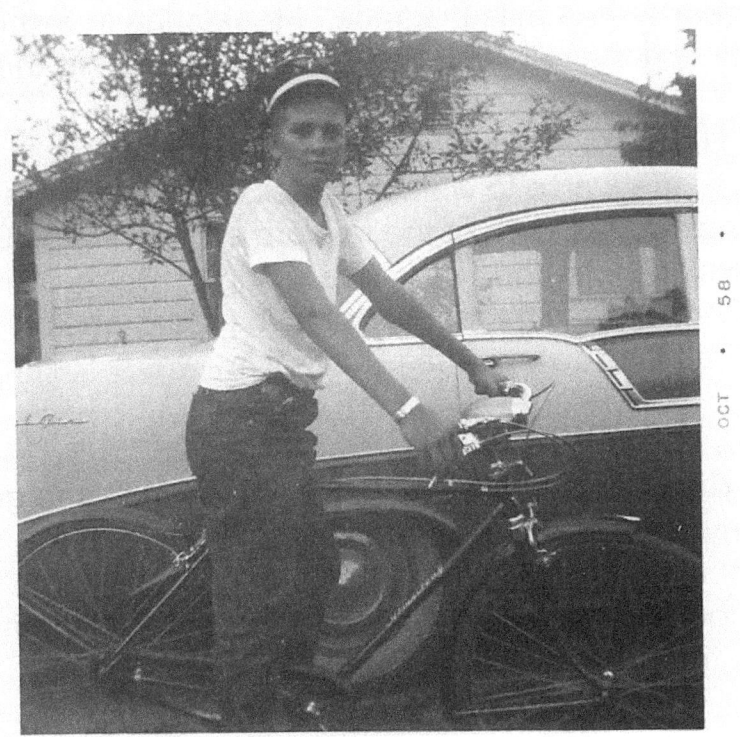

This is me on my English racer. Notice the 1956 Chevrolet and our house in the background. I was on a kick of wearing a boat captains hat, Where I got it I have no idea. The year was 1958.

Recollections of Raven & Richlands

I walked the rails most every day after I hit the track near home to the depot most every day. I literally walked a rail as I had trained myself to balance on it the full quarter of a mile distance. I took pride in being able to stay on the rail, as it had been my goal from the start.

The N & W railroad followed the Clinch River for miles. This made it nice to walk the tracks to our favorite fishing spots. Some of the favorite spots was the Curve, the Dixon Hole, the Ford, The Swinging Bridge, The Red Eye Hole, The mouth of Maynard's Branch and even as far down river as Daw. (Daw was a Railroad stop)

The Curve was the favorite place for the boys to go skinny dipping. It has been said that some of the curious teenage girls would slip up on the high bluff overlooking the rail road and river and watch the naked boys frolic in the Clinch.

Now I remember one tragic day when one of our playmates was carried off to Heaven right from Raven. The school bus had just let her and other kids off and a train was drawing near. The big horn of the train blew as usual at the crossing. The Johnson girl lived close to the tracks and was completely used to the noisy trains. She looked over toward the depot and saw someone over there she wanted to talk to. Oh! My Lord, she walked right into the path of that train and was carried right off to Heaven.

It was such a sad time to see one of our own taken in such a way. The Johnson family was so torn up. They ask us bigger boys to serve as pallbearers at the funeral. We were also at the house the night before, as back then folks took their dead home and had a wake. This was stamped into my memory so many years ago. I will never forget it. I remember the railroad folks kept the crossing warning lights on for several days as a tribute to Miss Johnson.

Now on a more positive note let me tell you about the last N & W passenger train run. I was in the 4th grade and the principal decided the whole school should enjoy this historic occasion as there would never be a train pulled by a steam locomotive again.

Oh! It was a fun day as all of us kids boarded the train; we were going to Saint Paul or Norton and make the run back to Raven.

I just about got into trouble that day along with a lot in our class. We decided it would be a lot of fun to kiss each other at every tunnel, maybe even other times. The principal was not happy about the report of our action. Nothing was ever done because there was no proof of whom or how many of us were involved. I do remember the little Reedy girl and I kissed a lot that day. I wonder if she remembers that.

The train track is a dangerous place if you are not alert. We boys would do the Indian test sometimes. The Indian test was simple, you would get down on your knees and place your ear right on the iron rail and listen. If there was a train coming within a mile or two you could hear it coming.

Speaking of danger, some men loved the Clinch River and loved to take their liquor to its banks and get drunk. Then in their drunken state they would decide to walk the track back home. There were several people killed and some close calls during those years.

Now this made us boys afraid to travel the railroad by night, because we were afraid of the ghosts, not the trains.

Colonel Charles Dahnmon Whitt

This is an N & W railroad Locomotive and crew.

Recollections of Raven & Richlands

This is a good look at the undercarriage of a steam powered N & W locomotive. Notice the size compared to the workman.

Colonel Charles Dahnmon Whitt

Powered by the fire spitting, stream squirting, smoke puffing N & W Engine.

This is the N & W RR Forman Section House in Richlands.
    Thought to be one of the oldest buildings in Richlands.

It is now going to be preserved and restored.

Colonel Charles Dahnmon Whitt

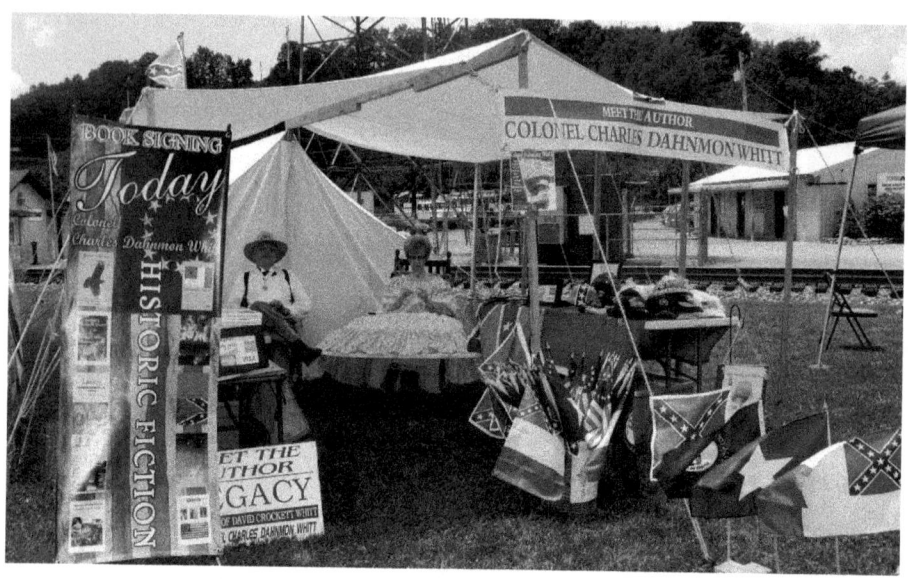

Colonel Whitt and Sharon sell books to help raise money to help the Section House Restoration Project.

Colonel Whitt & Sharon at Section House, 2013 Richlands Freedom Festival

Chapter 18
Parents & Grandparents

Like most folks raised in Raven I was privileged to have good God fearing parents and grandparents that raised me to be honest and hardworking, as well as to follow the Golden Rule.

With this chapter I am going back a bit to revisit my earliest years in Raven. My parents and grandparents had a profound impact on me, all in a positive manner.

My Grandpa Joseph Everett Fleming passed away when I was six years old. This was the first time that family death was so near to me. I do remember Grandpa, as a loving man that also made me feel safe. He had the qualities of a protector.

Grandpa Fleming and Grandma Lura Fleming bought a lot right next to us in Stinson Bottom. So I was around them for my first few years.

One thing that made me mention that Grandpa Fleming was protective was that I felt threatened by the Raven character, a Mr. Clines. This man was shabby and loafed around Raven and tried to scare children by

Colonel Charles Dahnmon Whitt

saying he would cut off their ears. One day Grandpa and I walked the railroad to the Raven Post Office to get the mail. On the way back we came in contact with Mr. Clines. Mr. Clines began his tactic to scare me and Grandpa took offense to this. He told the Clines man if he ever bothered me he would have to answer to him. Mr. Clines backed away and never bothered me again. Mr. Clines knew Grandpa's reputation of never backing down from a fight and that he was always carrying a loaded pistol. My grandpa carried a gun since his youth as he was brought up in the post-civil war era where feuds were prevalent. Grandpa was also known for his short Irish temper.

Grandpa Fleming like many folks in pre television days had a nice cabinet radio. It was multi band and would pick up radio signals from all over the world. The radio was his pride and joy and no one but he could touch it. I would sit with grandpa and listen to his radio. Grandpa would drink coffee, or sometimes, take out his pocket knife and cut a piece of tobacco from a Brown Mule plug.

The radio was about like the internet is to us today. They would offer things for sale and you could send a check or money order in and purchase them.

One day we heard about these balloon animals, so Grandpa wrote down the address and ordered some for me. I had pictured in my little head that they would look just like real animals. When they came in they were just balloons with ears or arms, but mostly just balloons.

The balloons came with cardboard feet that you attached so the balloons would stand up. This was before the plastic era.

I do remember grandpa saying that he would never order anything made by the Japs as it was junk. It was just after WW2 and it was fresh in his mind.

One day my dad ran next door to grandpa's house when grandma summoned him for help. I followed him to grandpa's house and when I got there grandpa was lying on the bed and dad was rubbing his arms and hands. Grandpa was not moving or talking.

Grandpa Fleming went to Heaven that day the 27th of May 1951. Back then folks brought their dead back home for the wake. I remember having Grandpa's casket in our living room and many people came to visit. The lightning bugs came early that year and that

Colonel Charles Dahnmon Whitt

night the fireflies were putting on a good demonstration for us. I wonder if they came early for Grandpa.

Grandma Lura Elizabeth Bellamy Fleming was a sweet lady and what you would think a grandma should be like. She lived several years after Grandpa passed. Grandma was particular how folks spelled and said her name, it was Lura. She would also tell folks she was from Old Virginia, not West Virginia.

Grandpa and grandma were both raised in the Clintwood area of Dickenson County. This was like the western frontier in the early part of 1900. People were self-reliant and helpful to their neighbors. Grandma was the oldest girl in her family and she learned to do many things. She could keep house, sew, garden, can food, make soap, gather wild greens and she even loved to fish. She has talked about her childhood and the things they did. Her mother was a widow and was born with one hand missing, yet they all survived and were good people.

Since grandma lived alone next to us after grandpa went to Heaven, grandma helped at our house. Mom went to work so grandma would watch after me and cook supper for dad and us kids. She sure knew how to

Recollections of Raven & Richlands

make good country meals. She made the best fried apple pies you ever tasted. Sometimes before supper, I would persuade her to give me a pie, if I promised to eat a good supper.

Grandma had hundreds of stories that a young boy would love to listen to. Indian stories, stories about fishing, stories about the civil war, and even big rattlesnake stories, to name a few. I am sure I could write a book just on her.

Now to talk just a little about my Grandpa Whitt; he struck me as a proud man, I think because he carried himself straight with good posture even after many years of hard work on the farm and in the coal mines.

I didn't get to know Grandpa Charles Henry Whitt too well. I did stop by and visit him from time to time after I was a teenager. I even took him fishing once when he was about 82. Now in the Raven area of the Clinch River, you do a lot of wade-fishing. I thought grandpa would sit on the bank. Heck no he waded right out in the river so he could fish around the rocks. I got in a little trouble with dad that evening when he found out I took grandpa fishing and let him get out in the river. There wasn't no letting him, he was a Whitt, and he went right out like I did.

Colonel Charles Dahnmon Whitt

Grandpa Whitt was my namesake; at least I got the Charles part of his name. Now I also have one son with the name of Charles.

Some of the things I remember about Grandpa Whitt are, he had a big red squirrel as a pet. He had a spring house that was set up to keep his milk, butter and other foods cool. I loved to go in there because he had a catfish in there that kept the spring house cleaned up. I thought that was great, grandpa having a catfish that worked for him. Grandpa also had a dried mushroom hanging over the door in a bedroom. He got it out of a coal mine and it was a scary thing. It was a good two feet long and looked just like a man's arm and hand. It was brown and it had a thumb and 4 fingers even though some of the fingers looked to be flattened out. I always thought it was a ghost arm and hand.

The Whitt's seem to be jack of all trades and Grandpa Whitt was typical. He could play music on his old pump organ and also on a piano. He played by ear and could play most of the old songs. One I remember especially was, "Little Brown Jug."

Grandpa even took up photography back in the early part of 1900. Of course that was the day with the big box camera with the big black cloth over your head.

He bought his house in 1910, just below the Old White Church. He paid $1000.00 for the house and a couple of acres. Grandpa and Grandma Amanda Elizabeth (Mandy) Puckett Whitt had 5 kids by 1920 when she went to Heaven with the flu epidemic. Of course I never saw Mandy, because I didn't come along until 1944.

Liller Lee Simmons Whitt, the second wife of Charles Henry Whitt. She is taking a little nap it seems at their home just below the Old White Church. I liked the ad on the thermometer.

Amanda Elizabeth Puckett Whitt, "Mandy"
Wonderful Lady I have been told.

Colonel Charles Dahnmon Whitt

According to her pictures she was a beautiful lady. She got the flu by going and waiting on the sick neighbors round about.

Now grandpa had five kids to raise so he married quick to a much younger lady. Her Name was Liller Lee Simmons and that made her my step-grandma.

Grandpa and his new wife started having kids and before long had five. Of course these were my uncles and one aunt, not too much older than my brothers and I.

When I was still small dad and mom went to Mississippi to pick up one of my uncles that was in the service there. My brothers and I stayed with Grandpa Whitt while they were gone. He still used his fire places' for heat and piled on big layers of heavy quilts to keep you warm.

It was a fun time at Grandpa's. When dad and mom got back with my uncle they had a lot to tell us. While traveling away from the mountains down in the flatlands of Mississippi they kept seeing signs along the road advertising "Pizza Pie". Now dad and mom had never heard of pizza pie so they imagined it to be some wonderful fruit pie like apple or fruit or even a custard pie. They were hungry and decided to stop and get some pizza pie. They were shocked at the site of this new food but they really enjoyed it. Pizza Pie finally made it into the mountains of southwest Virginia.

Edith Lyle Fleming Whitt About 1934

Dad and mom were married on September 14, 1935. Dad had a job with the Raven Red Ash Coal Company and was 22 years old. Mom was just 16 and still living at home with her mom and dad Fleming.

My Parents
Edith Lyle Fleming Whitt & Marvin Bertran Whitt
Young Love around 1935

Recollections of Raven & Richlands

My mom Edith Lyle Fleming was of Irish descent and was quick tempered. You might say she was like an old momma bears when it came to protecting her children. One example of this I remember was the time my Brother Larry was kept after school. Jerry came home without Larry. Mom asked, Jerry where Larry was and he told mom that the teacher kept him after school. Mom didn't like the report but didn't say much.

Next day after school Jerry came home without Larry again. Mom asked Jerry where Larry was. Jerry told mom that the teacher kept Larry after school again. Mom said, "I will just see about that," as she huffed out to the old car and away she went.

It was not long, Mom and Larry was back. Larry was never retained after school again. I bet mom scared the britches off of that teacher. When she was mad she was a hand full.

My mom was very smart, after we were all up in school she went to the Licensed Practical Nurse School offered by the Clinch Valley Clinic.

Mom only went through the 7th grade, but she came out second in her class at LPN nursing school.

Mom had a great reputation as a good nurse, all of her Patients loved her. She worked for years at both the

Clinch Valley Clinic and also at the Mattie Williams Hospital in Richlands as well as private duty.

Mattie Williams Hospital

This is the old hospital I spent a week in with Spinal Meningitis. My Dr. Thompson tapped my spin and drew out some liquid. He did it with one arm as he had an arm paralyzed in the war. Prayers to God saved me.

Dad Marvin B. Whitt, Uncles Ralph Whitt, and David Eugene Whitt
Picture was taken in front of the Old Whitt House, just below the Old White Church. The road is old Route 67. Notice the Old car coming down the road.

Colonel Charles Dahnmon Whitt

Dad was a hard working coal miner; he always came home with a coal blackened face from his days work.

Most of the men around Raven made their living working underground getting the coal out to fuel the nation.

Dad was a good provider and always made sure we had clothes, food and all the things that we needed. He also was a Christian father that made sure we went to church. Dad was pretty strict with us and he taught us to work and carry our load.

Dad always put out big gardens and raised extra corn to feed the hogs and sometimes a calf he would fatten up for us to eat. You guessed it, we all learned about hoeing in the garden and all that went with growing our food. Dad had good luck with his crops I guess you could say he had a green thumb.

Dad was a praying man, I remember when I was small I could hear him praying every night as he kneeled by his bed to talk to God. Some of you may disagree with me, but I think dad was the best man I ever knew.

Recollections of Raven & Richlands

Dad was a Sunday school superintendent and a Lay Speaker at the Raven Methodist Church. Back then our church was on a circuit with other churches which meant that the pastor would rotate between churches. This left a vacancy at our church on some Sundays. Many times dad would fill the pulpit.

Dad did not have much spare time but he would try to spend time with us. Back in those day families loved Sunday drives, picnics, fishing, and even a shopping trip to get school clothes or Christmas gifts. We would motor to Bluefield on the West Virginia line or to Bristol which was on the Tennessee line.

I think I could write another book just on my parents and grandparents, but I will not say much more in this collection. I will add that most parents were much like mine; they were God fearing and patriotic people that loved their family.

Of course in every culture you have the loafer and the grasshopper type people. Most in Raven were of the ant type of people; always working and trying to get ahead for their families.

Chapter 19
SON OF A COAL MINER

My Daddy was a Coal Miner!

If he came home early with a clean face, I knew he had a treat for me.

I would run to meet him so I could get the goodies from his round dinner bucket.

He would have a baloney sandwich and maybe some fruit. If I was lucky there would be a little cake too.

I did not know the trouble and dangers Daddy went through for me.

He would come home with a black face of love; it had to be given to him from God above.

He was surely a man of God and had many Guardian Angels.

One day the angels were surely busy protecting other miners and a great rock fell on my Daddy.

He prayed and talked to the men trying to make him free.

He did not faint away and he told them what to do. They shored up the roof, but the rock was too big to move.

Daddy was on a Motor* so he rocked himself free.
(A battery powered flat vehicle used by mine foreman.)

They put Daddy in a rough riding truck; on across the rough road they went with their precious cargo.

When the doctor was through he just shook his head. Then the doctor said, "It's a wonder you ain't dead!"

Daddy broke his pelvis and seven ribs and his collar bone too. God was watching and saved his life that day.

Daddy was a Coal Miner and I am so proud.

The Guardian Angels stayed close for years until Jesus came to take him home at age 94.

So if your Daddy comes home from work with a black face, it is no disgrace.

My Daddy was a Coal Miner and I love him so.

Chapter 20
Boy Scouts

Dahnmon in the Boy Scouts 1959.

Recollections of Raven & Richlands

Stinson Bottom, Raven VA

The Boy Scouts of America had a good impact on me as I grew into manhood. I think I was in the 6th grade when I learned about a new Boy Scout troop forming at the new Assembly of God Church in Raven. The Pastor was W. W. Smith and he ended up being a friend to all of us boys. I remember going to dad and asking him if I could join. Back then your dad was the leader and Authoritarian in the family. Dad asked me several questions and finally said yes if I would do better in school. I remember going and the room was filled with noisy boys. We learned the first meeting to shut up when Preacher Smith, (as we called him.) held up his arm and hand in the Scout sign.

I got a copy of the Boy Scout handbook and brought it home to show dad. He looked it over and said that it was a good book with good teaching in it. He also said that if I would read the book it would actually help me in school. That little book was a great help to me, because it was interesting to me. To pass Tenderfoot and get your first badge you had to learn the Scout Oath, The Scout Law, the Scout slogan and the Scout Motto. I quickly mastered this and I didn't just memorize it, I still can quote it all word for word to this day.

Colonel Charles Dahnmon Whitt

When I see young boys in the Scout Uniform I often start quoting the Oath and Law to them. This usually brings some smiles from the boys and even their Scout leaders.

Our Scoutmaster, Preacher Smith, was a great scout leader. He wanted all of us boys to learn about the Lord, be patriotic, and learn things that would help us throughout our entire lives. We started right off going on camping trips and learning skills of the outdoors. We learned to cook in the outdoors by, how to build our fires and be safe. We learned that you did not cook on a raging fire, but you let it die down a bit. You raked some nice hot coals to one side and cooked on the more even heat. We got pretty good at it. We discovered it was possible to cook your meat all the way through without burning the outside. We learned about pitching tents and the best place to do that. We learned to set up camp on raised ground so when the rains came down, the tents would not flood.

We learned about the scout uniform and what it all meant, we learned the value of earning our badges. If we couldn't swim, we learned. We even learned about First-Aid, just to be prepared. After all the Boy Scout Motto is, "Be prepared."

Recollections of Raven & Richlands

The things I learned in scouting have benefitted me through the years. We learned to think ahead, that is good in any job. We learned to prepare for any obstacle. That too is good for any job. We learned to get along and work as a team that too is a good thing in any job; all of these things are good for life.

We formed friendships in scouting and bonded with our buddies which have lasted unto this day. I have found out that the boys from Raven were raised right at home and this made them even better Boy Scouts.

We took weeklong camping trips every summer, we explored mountain tops, and we went under the earth in the caves like Chimney Cave on Claypool Hill. As I think back I believe that Preacher Smith was the biggest duck in the puddle as he led us into all the exciting places we went.

Our Scout troop raised money and took in donation. We even took in an abandoned house and airplane hangar. We tore these down with the skills we learned by using tools. The lumber was saved to build our new scout house.

Colonel Charles Dahnmon Whitt

Preacher Smith was a builder and fine carpenter. After all he had led the building of the new Assembly of God Church in Raven.

We gathered some old telephone poles and sank them in the ground as a foundation for our Scout house. We wanted it up off the ground because we built it in the flood plain on the back of the church property. It was almost on the bank of the Clinch River. If I remember correctly it stood about six to seven feet above the ground. It was a grand scout house, it was spacious and we even had a fire pit with a hood and chimney pipe to take out the smoke. I don't know if it still stands today or not.

I need to mention that Preacher Smith taught us how to build fires by friction and flint and steel. After we mastered that he would not allow us to take matches on any of our outings. We took that as a challenge.

Some of the boy's name that belonged to the Raven troop was Cordle, Shelton, Grose, Welch, Lane, Lawson, Whitt and several others during the time the Raven troop was active.

Recollections of Raven & Richlands

Let me tell you about one of our week long trips. While the Raven Scout Troop was camping at the park on High Knob Mountain near Coeburn Virginia, It rained like a monsoon. After a day and two nights of staying in leaky pup tents, our Scout Master W.W. Smith had enough! He went to a phone to call a friend that had a hunter's cabin on out the mountain in some of the most primitive land east of the Mississippi River. The man told Preacher Smith that he was welcome to take the troop to the cabin, and relayed the location of the hidden key.

We broke camp that wet morning, loaded up our wet stuff and headed out for another new adventure. Back in those days deer and other game was scarce, but not on High Knob. Most of us had never seen a deer out in the wild before. As we traveled out the little mountain road we counted over twenty deer as we passed.

Guess what, the rain stopped as we came up on the little cabin. As we got out of the little bus, the first thing we saw in the soft ground was, *bear tracks*! Wow! This sent fear abounding into every boy there, and probably our Scout Master too! Of course he tried to calm our souls by telling us that a bear would not bother a bunch of noisy boys. This did not help us too much!

Colonel Charles Dahnmon Whitt

We moved into the cabin with all our gear. There were about a dozen of us. We only had enough floor space for all the boys to lie down.

There was no water or plumbing, so Preacher Smith (Scoutmaster) told me and Frankie to stay at the cabin and watch our stuff, while he took all the other boys on an expedition to look for drinking water.

After all the boys left, Frankie and I were quite scared there by ourselves. We were both church goers and I had a little Bible in my gear. I don't remember how I knew about the 91st Psalms, but I turned there and begin to read God's word!

The 91st Psalm is all about how God gives his followers protection. This was soothing to our souls, in a time of distress. After reading the word Frankie and I had a little prayer meeting up on the mountain sitting there in that little cabin. We were still alert, but were not so scared after our talk with God.

It wasn't long before we heard a commotion as all the boys came running back to the cabin. They had had a frightful encounter with a large *black bear* out in the woods.

Recollections of Raven & Richlands

They gave us a report that they came up on him and he lowered his head and extended his neck while letting out a loud growl. The bruin never offered to back up or run. This was his mountain and he would defend it if it came to that. The boys panicked and ran in different directions all leading to the shelter of the hunter's cabin! Preacher Smith tried not to show alarm, but was on the heels of the running scouts.

We all decided we did not want to build a fire outside of the cabin to cook our suppers. So we all sit in the cabin eating various canned foods cold and right out of the cans. I never will forget I opened a can of spaghetti, dumped it into my surplus mess kit which had some spilled soap powders in it. I never noticed the soap until I begin to eat. I ate around the soap the best I could. It was not a good meal.

Our Scout Master tried to act brave and even said he was going to put his sardine can outside the door to attract the bear. He was always fooling with us like that. I did notice he stayed in the cabin with the rest of us.

We had a restless night and when we got up to go outside for latrine purposes, the first thing we saw was fresh bear tracks that led to the cabin! That insolent bruin had followed the running scouts right to the cabin! Needless to say we were alert that morning.

Our Scout Master decided to move us one more time. He knew about a church camp over in Lee County, Virginia that was open and not too far away. We never let on about being scared, but none complained about packing up and heading off the mountain and wilds of High Knob.

This was just another time in my young life that I called upon the God of Creation in a time of fear and trouble.

Recollections of Raven & Richlands

Marvin and Dahnmon 1956
Hunger Mother's Park

Colonel Charles Dahnmon Whitt

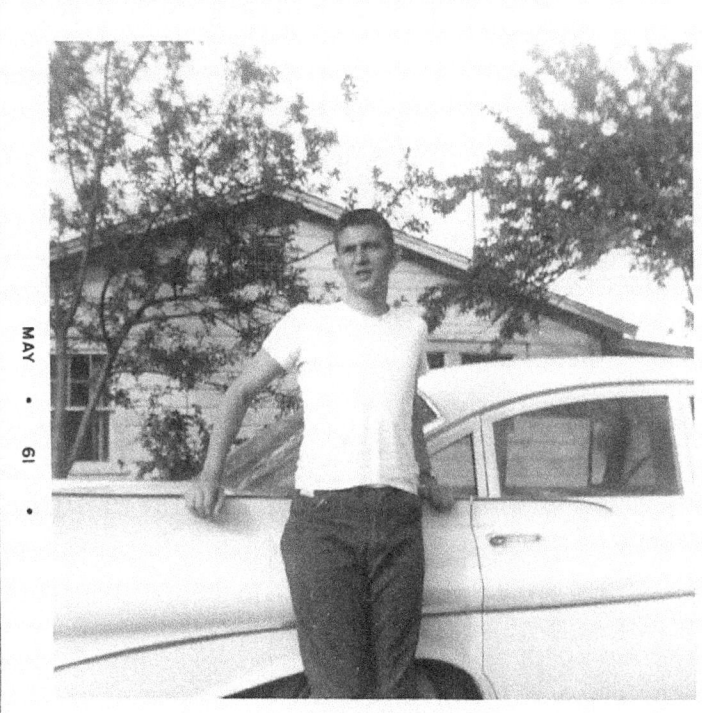

Dahnmon and Dad's 59 Pontiac
I learned to drive on this 1959 Pontiac, I heard Dad say, "I'm not going to turn that kid loose with a $3000.00 car. Ha! It was new when he said that. Looked at a new car price lately?

Recollections of Raven & Richlands

Chapter 21
The Raven Super Market

Back in December of 1962 my mom informed me that I had a job at the Raven Super Market. It was just for the Christmas season for now she told me. I had never had a steady job up to this point except my paper route. Of course I did little things to make a buck here and there. I was a little nervous about working in that big store with so much to learn.

My mom had talked to A. W. Horton Jr. (Nick Name June.) about hiring me and he said he could use some extra help over Christmas and to send me in. After I arrived I saw a good friend of mine, Jim Butcher, and he would show me around and help me learn the ropes. I felt more at ease already.

Now let me tell you a little about the Raven Super Market. I have been told that they there had been a store there before called McCall's. I think it burned down or maybe torn down to build the Raven Super Market. Now the term super market usually makes you think of a big grocery store. The Raven Supermarket was and is a giant general store. Back in 1962 about one third of the store all on the left side was dedicated to groceries, they carried most food and canned items

and also had a big meat counter in the back. They offered roasts, pork chops and sliced meats. You simply went to the counter and someone would help you with your order.
They kept processed meats that you could have sliced also: ham, chopped ham, bologna, cheese, and many other things.

Yes, I learned to be a half-way butcher. I sliced meat and wrapped it in the white paper and tied it with string. I also chopped the pork chops using the big butcher knife and meat cleaver. Some of my pork chops looked like they had been cut with a rock. No one ever complained.
They had a big butcher block to work on; it was the first one I ever saw. It was a big heavy block of solid wood about 4 feet by 4 feet and about that high. It was the biggest piece of wood I ever saw beside some big trees in the woods.

Back then soda pop was still in glass bottles and that was part of my duties, to take them and store them for the pop man. Sometimes I would find a bottle of pop that came in to be sold and it would have old rotten peanuts in it. That was a thing we Raven people used to do. We would buy a bag of peanuts, and a Coke or

RC and pour our peanuts in the pop. Then as we drank the pop we would eat a nut or two. Sometimes the bottling company scrubbers failed to get the nuts out. I would always save these nasty looking pops and give them back to the pop man for a free pop.

The grocery side also had a dairy cooler for milk, butter, and the like. While I worked there the great invention of putting biscuits in a paper tube came out. Some of the folks would come and shop and loaf around Raven for a spell. Those cans of biscuits would get warmed up and start popping and we called it a young war. Anything to laugh about was our thinking.
That just about covered the grocery part of the big store.

Now that left two thirds of the space for everything else at the Raven Super Market. They carried most everything that the Raven and Richlands folks would need. They kept coal miners supplies such as knee pads, Wheat Brand battery lights, carbide lights, heavy belts and whatever else a coal miner would need including the Miners hard hats.

They carried boots and shoes from steel toed to Sunday loafers. They carried clothing from bib overalls to casual dress. They carried all types of hardware from nails to tools, to you name it. They carried fishing rods and reels and all the tackle any fisherman would need.

June Horton took care of trading in guns; he kept pistols shotguns, and high powered rifles. Back then before President Kennedy was killed the gun laws were very lax. You could buy new guns or used guns, even trade guns. I do have to mention one incident about gun traders. One evening a man came in the front door and June was near the front. The man held the gun pointing up for safety. He asked June if he would look at the pistol and give him a price on it for a trade or outright buy. June always asked, "Is it loaded?" The man told June that he would ever carry a loaded pistol in to your store. June took the pistol in his hand pointed it up and pulled the trigger. Bang! That thing went off and shot a hole in the ceiling. June got all over the man. The man actually thought it was empty. There are more folks shot with empty guns than with loaded guns it seems.

They carried all types of cooking ware, especially the good old cast iron skillets. Do you get the idea it was truly a super market. They carried dough rollers, and so many things too numerous to mention. If a Raven area person wanted something by chance they didn't have June would order it and it would come in on the train or

Recollections of Raven & Richlands

the next truck.

They even carried fencing and garden supplies, seeds and all. In spring you could get your baby chickens there. That was part of my duty, to feed and care for the biddies. We kept them under a light to keep them warm. Sometimes some would die over night; I would have to get them out. The little rascals would stink and even get rotten overnight. I would light up my pipe with Cherry Blend tobacco and get them out. Sometimes their legs would pull off. Wow enough about that.

About smoking my pipe, I have a quick story to tell you. You see my dad did not know that I had taken up smoking my pipe. One evening I had my pipe smoking like a freight train as I swept up the aisles getting ready to close. I looked up and there stood dad. He had a little crooked grin on his face. If I could have swallowed that pipe I would have.

When I first went to work I was really green about working in the store. If you think back you will remember I missed playing store in the first grade. I remember the first time I made a sale and had to work the old Dayton Cash Register and give back change. Now in those days the register would not tell the clerk how much change to give back. June was watching me

Colonel Charles Dahnmon Whitt

as I stood there trying to figure in my head about how much change the patron would get. June was a great boss and he simply told me how to do it. He explained that you take the price of the item and count up to the amount of the money rendered. A light bulb lit up in my mind and I never had a problem to this day giving back change.

I worked all through Christmas selling toys and things like Radio flyer bikes, wagons, sleighs, and all the items that Santa would have under the tree on Christmas for all the good little Raven kids. In Raven most Christmas Trees were Cedar in those days because they were abundant in the area.

Now I liked working at the Raven Super Market and June decided to keep me on through inventory and I stayed there on up until I left for the Navy in July 1964.

Jim and I loved to kid each other, but Jim tricked me first. We were working together counting this and that for inventory when we came up on this big nail ben. Jim never cracked a smile as he told me to start counting the nails. I looked back with a funny look on my face and he laughed out loud. We either weigh or estimate stuff like that he explained.

Recollections of Raven & Richlands

Jim and I became real good friends at work and off. We double dated, went on fishing trips and even to the football games together. He always could get his dad's beautiful 1960 turquoise Chevy for out running around.

One of our duties was to deliver groceries, hog chop in those 100 pound printed cloth sacks, (The country ladies loved the material the sacks were made of.) and other thing all the way up to big Warm Morning coal stoves. We had, I think a three quarter ton 1950 Studebaker pickup to use. June would not drive it so it was up to us. It was a stiff old truck and very hard to drive. The transmission was not synchronized and you had to be stopped to get into first gear and the clutch was also tricky.

Remember I said Jim and I were both pranksters, one day Jim was driving up the big hill now called Young Road. It is a steep hill and the old Studebaker was in groaning up the hill. Out of the blue I reached over and pulled the big emergency brake handle and stalled us. Jim looked at me so funny.

"What did you do that for?" he said with a serious voice.

I was laughing so hard at the look on his face and he

Colonel Charles Dahnmon Whitt

knew I had got one over on him. We both laughed as the old truck jumped and carried on trying to get started up the steep hill again. Those were the good old days.

I had known June and his family all my life as they went to the Raven Methodist Church with us. "Rocky" was June's son, I think A.W. Horton the third. He was mostly just a kid in the early days when I worked the store. Rocky was always hanging around and playing in the store. He didn't know it at the time but June was teaching Rocky the ropes of running a big store. Now over the years Rocky has run the Raven Super Market and still does. Jane Ellen, June's daughter grew up to be a fine lady and continues to be my friend.

I was at the Raven Super Market last summer and walked all through the store with my wife. Rocky has made some changes over the years. There is little food items sold there now but much more hardware.

June was a real good boss, I have to say it was the best job I ever had. I learned so much about working and about life. There was never any pressure on me the whole time I worked there.

Now in Raven, right across the street is another land

Recollections of Raven & Richlands

mark. The Raven Drug store is still in business after so many years. It used to be a hang out for us younger folks. They had a soda fountain and I drank many Cherry Smashes there with my friends.

Now another childhood friend started working at the Raven Drug Store way back. His name is Danny Harris. Danny went on to pharmacy school and came back to fill prescriptions and now after so many years he owns the Raven Drug Store. Danny has kept it up and done remodeling and it is a showplace in Raven.

One quick story about Danny, as I said we went to school together up on School House Hill. One Christmas I got a set of boxing gloves and couldn't wait to try them out. The first day back to school after being on Christmas break; I took my boxing gloves with me to school. The first boy to box me was Danny Harris, heck it didn't take him a minute to bloody my nose. This all happened before school started. Danny was very sorry, but I learned a lesson that morning. That was the good old days.

If you have never been to the Raven Super Market, you must go and see this Raven landmark. Rocky keeps it open and well stocked. You will see things there that you have not seen in years. It is a good place to shop for just about anything. If Rocky don't have it, tell him and odds are he can get it for you just like his dad did for all of those years. Tell Rocky that Dahnmon Whitt sent you.

(Maybe Rocky will give you a discount.)

Recollections of Raven & Richlands

Chapter 22
Richlands High School

My time, 8th Grade thru 12th Grade 1959 to 1964

Colonel Charles Dahnmon Whitt

It was the Tuesday after Labor Day, 1958. I was up and dressed and walked up the dusty gravel road to the old white church. The church was a school bus stop. I was now in the 8th grade and would be going to school with the big boys and girls. Yes due to space, the 8th grade class was added to the high school classes.

The invention of the middle school had not made its way to Tazewell County, Virginia by 1958. Also the State of Virginia had mandated the twelve year school system. Just before this, the students only went eleven years to public school. They went 1-7 in grade school and 8-11 in high school. The 1958-1959 school term was the first year of the twelve year education system. I was not real happy about that. It seemed I would go to school all of my life.

Now school students have social class' as well as age classes'. The 8th grad was the lowest of the pecking order in Richlands High.

My bus filled with 8th to 12th graders arrived in front of the school and the driver opened the door, seemingly wanting to get rid of his load as soon as possible. I got off the bus and looked around. Students were all standing outside for the doors to open. Many of them were standing around smoking cigarettes. This was a new sight for me as well.

The next thing was when William "Bill" Powers opened the big doors that led into the school and the gym. I heard his booming voice saying everyone go to the gym. I know this man meant business from the tone of his voice. The teachers were also on hand to herd all of us to the gym. It reminded me of officers in the military, (the teachers as officers,) and us as the privates. We all headed up in to the bleachers but the buzzing of all the students could still be heard. The upper classmen were used to this but we 8th graders were lost so we just followed.

As the last of the students took seats in the bleachers, Mister Powers booming voice was heard instructing us to be quiet. He had no microphone and did not need one. Two boys mocked with some back talk, Mister Powers took instant action. He knew the two and called them by name. He instructed them to go and wait for him at his office. The place got instantly quiet, because all of us knew that Mister Powers meant business and the two boys were already regretting their mischief. They would feel the presence of the board of education real soon.

As everyone got quiet, teachers one at a time came out

Colonel Charles Dahnmon Whitt

and read a list of names. She was what they call a homeroom teacher. When she finished with her list she spoke in a commanding voice. Follow me to room so and so. These kids would follow her and that would be their homeroom for the school term. This was new to me and all the 8th graders. We would have a home room and a different teacher for each subject class. Up to now we all had a single teacher for the full day and she taught us all of the subjects.

My name was finally called and I joined a group of kids on the gym floor. After my teacher finished the list we followed her to the class room. In the class room, she addressed us and welcomed us to Richlands High School. She continued by giving us a sheet of paper with all of our classes and times and room numbers. She explained that each morning we were to get off the bus and at the start of school we were to be in that room and in our seats. We would have a little time to catch up on homework, listen to the announcements, devotion, and a prayer to start off our day. Our homeroom teacher would be a friend and help us with our questions. She also assigned us our lockers and basically gave us other important information.

That first day, we would not stay all day, but would go to

Recollections of Raven & Richlands

each of our classes, meet our teachers, get assignment and the name of the text book we would need for that class. It was the responsibility of each student to provide his or her own text books. In most cases the 8th graders could purchase a used book from an upper classman. Being 8th graders I think we had to buy almost all of our books new. I remember that first day was very confusing to me. The big building and all the bigger students out in the halls at the same time made it tough to navigate to each class. That first day we also learned about the bell system. One bell was to get up and walk in a normal as possible manner and find the next class room, the second bell went off we were to be in our seats. We had five minutes to go to our locker, get what we needed for the next class and get to it. Of course we would try to socialize with our friends when we could. No one and Mister Powers proclaimed that no one would be out running the halls after that second bell.

I made it that first day, remembered the bus number and got on it back to Raven. After getting hollered at by our grumpy bus driver we were all dropped off from Richlands to Doran to the Old White Church in Raven. It was kind a tough getting accustomed to the new school and all that went with it. I did notice one good thing on my schedule, we had a lunch period. They reminded us that we needed to bring a quarter each day to pay for lunch. Now in Raven school I loved recess and lunch. Here at Richlands we had no recess but we did have physical education and lunch. I like both of them.

I noticed right off that the upper classmen were always looking down on all of us smaller 8th graders. It was more or less a social order at the school. Even in our own group, the 8th graders had social groups. Why kids do this I have no idea unless they are stupid and think they are better than everyone else. Kids from Richlands Elementary and Cedar Bluff Elementary, not all, but some looked down on kids from Raven, Red Ash, Jewell Ridge or Bandy. It seemed that as the time went on, things leveled off. People found out that kids from Raven were just as smart as they were. Some of the smartest kids and athletes came from Raven.

In recent years the county has talked about closing the Raven School. But when the kids take their tests they beat all of the other county elementary schools.

Now after some time I made many friends at Richlands High School. Some have become lifelong friends. As for learning at Richlands High, we did just that. As I think back, I realize that I got a much better education than I first believed. The teachers were conscientious and took time to help us learn. Richlands has turned out students that went on to college and became doctors and nurses. Some went to trade schools while many like me, went into the military. Vietnam was raging when I got out of school. I volunteered for the Navy. As it turned out that really helped me to finish growing up and becoming a good citizen I think. Vietnam took several of the finest men from Richlands High School. One of the things I really enjoyed in Richlands High was the fact that there were lots of pretty girls there. I was at the age I began noticing such beauty. The school provided for us a way to be social. There was dancing after football games, the prom, football games, basketball games and even some special dances. Lots of times buses would be run to carry the students to the out of town games. I claimed several girls for my girlfriends in high school. Of course some were more special than others. Some of the going steady relationships didn't last very long. I dropped some girls and some girls dropped me. Until you had a car and a driver's license, it was hard to see your girlfriends. Some lived way cross the county. The fire died out pretty quick when you never saw each other.

After we got over the initial shock of going to high school we began to bond together and were proud of

Colonel Charles Dahnmon Whitt

the Richlands Blue Tornadoes. That was our name in all sports and events. Don't ask me how they came up with that name. I think Richlands Blue Tornadoes was the only tornado within one hundred miles of the school. You don't get many tornados in the mountains of Virginia. In 2014 we will have our fifty year reunion and I still pull for the Blue Tornados, Some folks call them the "Blues." I like the name, "Blue Tornadoes" much better.

Like Raven School, Richlands High had to go to the stagger system with two shifts and all the students overlapped at lunch time. I think we all got a good education regardless of the shorter days. I remember I would get out of school at 2:20 each day and drive my 1953 Pontiac down to Raven and work each evening at the Raven Super Market until I graduated and went off to the Navy.

VISITOR—Apprentice Charles D. Whitt, son of Mr. and Mrs. Marvin Whitt, of Raven, has been visiting his parents for the past two weeks. He recently completed basic training at the Naval Training Center, San Diego, Calif. He has been assigned to the Aviation Electronic Technician School in Memphis. Charles is a 1964 graduate of Richlands High School.

Chapter 23
Leaving For The Navy

I was still in high school and in my senior year I began in earnest contemplating what I would do after graduation. I was tired of school and was ready to do something else. I wanted a job or something besides more school. I did not even consider going to college. I doubt at that time that I wouldn't go if I was well paid. That was my state of mind. I talked to some of my friends, and many of them were considering joining the military. Now the Viet Nam war was going on and many of our boys had been drafted. I was classified as IV-A with the Selective Service. Those of you not familiar with the draft, IV-A is the next up to be drafted. I thought that the Air Force or Navy would be a better way to go. It had always been in the back of my mind to join the Navy.

My Dad had talked about wanting to be in the Navy and I think that must have been why I chose it. I didn't know a single thing about the U.S. Navy, heck I thought they wore those pretty Cracker-Jack Blue uniforms all the time. Dad had tried to join after WW-1 but they had cut back and would only put him on a waiting list. Later when WW_2 came along Dad was married and had 2 kids. He was also a coal miner so he never went to war. Coal was in great demand to run the war factories and power the Navy's war ships.

I went to see the Navy recruiter just to find out what they offered. Of course the other military branch recruiters were on hand and standing around like vultures wanting to jump on some new dead meat. I made my way to the Navy guy.

He greeted me warmly and we sat down to talk. The first questions were where did I go to school and how were my grades? I had to be honest so I told him that I was smarter than my grades reflected. I had not really tried to excel in high school. I got by, was my reply. Well he looked a little doubtful at me and told me what would be next. He explained that I would go through a full day of testing and I would be offered my best chance after the scores came back.

The recruiter set me up with testing along with other young men. He picked me up early in the morning and then picked up four more young men and drove us to Beckley West Virginia for our tests.

In a few days the recruiter called me and was quite excited to meet with me again. He came to our home to

Colonel Charles Dahnmon Whitt

fill out more papers and talk about what "This Man's Navy" could do for me.

The recruiter was well pleased with all of my scores. He explained that I had scored highly on all of my tests and had to admit that he was somewhat dumbfounded after looking at my grade transcript. He explained to me that the other four lads that took the test with me had all been A and B students and I had beaten all of them.

The recruiter proudly told me that I was able to choose any school the Navy offered and that he recommended electronics and Nuclear Submarine service school. My first question was how long do I have to sign up for? He said I would be going to school for two years so I would have to sign up for six years. I quickly answered back with what else could I have? He asked what I liked to do. I said I like girls and fishing. He laughed and said I would fit in with the Navy just fine, but what were some of my hobbies? I told him that I loved to build the big wooden airplane models and fly them. His next question was, do you think you would like to be in aviation? That sounded much better than going under the water in a submarine. Yes I think that would be an interesting thing to go after, but how long do I have to sign up for? He laughed and said you can get that if you sign up for four years.

Recollections of Raven & Richlands

Next he said if I would go ahead and sign up while I was still in school I could pick the day I would leave, of course after graduation. He said he could also give me a choice of boot camp locations, Great Lakes Illinois, or San Diego California.

After talking it over with Dad and Mom, I decided to sign up. They both seemed to be pleased with the idea. I had never been to the west coast and was not sure if I would ever have that chance again so I would choose San Diego and would wait until July to leave. This would give me time to take our senior trip to Washington D.C. and also to the World's Fair in New York City. It would allow me to go to the prom, and even give me a month or so after school to give me a vacation. I signed up and finished all that was ahead of me including my work at the Raven Super Market. After graduation I gave notice to June Horton, and by this time he knew I would be leaving for the Navy. I wanted to do some fishing, and loafing, and spend some time with a girlfriend before I flew off to boot camp.

I have to tell you this little story. It was my last fishing adventure before I left for the Navy. I decided to go fishing and not work at it. I wanted to go to some still waters and cast out some bait and just lay back and

Colonel Charles Dahnmon Whitt

take it all in. I could just walk from our house, cross the Mill Creek Bridge like heading to Simmons Town and Long Branch. Follow the gravel road to the railroad and follow the railroad to one of my favorite fishing holes. It was a long wide, pool in the Clinch River known by Raven people as the Dixon Hole. It was a nice sunny June morning and the walk was enjoyable. I did not have a care in the world as I came to the high bank overlooking the Dixon Hole. I made my way down the bank, baited my hook with a big fat night crawler and cast it out into the deep. I set my pole on a green fork that I had cut from a branch on the river bank. I sat back and began to take it all in. The upper part of the Dixon Hole was an eddy as the narrow river flowed into the wide expanse of the river. The water in the Dixon hole moved slowly because of its wide boundaries. It was a good day to be alive, and I really didn't care if I caught a fish or not. I just wanted to relax and be one with nature before I traveled to unknown adventures of boot camp.

Now where I was sitting below the high bank I could hear if a train came by or if a car traveled the gravel road as both were behind me. I was sitting there sort of day dreaming and letting my thoughts drift about, just like the slow waters of the Clinch in front of me. I could understand the words of the Twenty Third Psalms when it spoke of beside of still waters.

I had sat there long enough to get comfortable and was enjoying the serenity of God's green earth when I heard several voices and walking coming from the railroad behind me. What is this all about I asked myself. There seems to be too many to be other fishermen and too many to be drunks. I didn't have to wait too long before I knew. Several men appeared on the bank above me and I heard one man say, "Looks like he had been lying in these weeds and rolled over the bank."

Then they made their way down the steep bank and were very concentrated on their task. One man walked to the edge of the river just ten feet away and bent down and picked up a pocket knife. He turned to the others and said, "Look, here is his knife!"

No one even acknowledged that I was sitting there fishing. I looked at the men and realized that they were members of the rescue squad. Some had ropes with grappling hooks and they even carried a row boat down the bank. At this time I was still sitting there fishing, but when they started throwing their hooks into the Clinch and dragging them back I realized I better get my line out of the water and get out of their way. I knew it was not going to be a rescue, but a recovery they were trying to do. I stood back out of the way and asked a few questions and they told me what they suspected. There was a man we all knew that loved to lie around the river and drink his liquor and he had another problem. He was a diabetic. Drinking and low sugar are a good combination to do you in. I knew the man and can relate to a time I ran into him and the county deputy on the railroad. The man was just about to go into a coma when I got there, the deputy gave me a dime and told me to run to the Raven Super Market and get some red cherry pop and get my ass back as quick as possible. I did as I was told and the deputy poured the sweet pop down his throat and he began to come out of it. Now it appears that same man had done the same thing on the bank of the Clinch and rolled into eternity.

It was late in the day before the man's body was recovered. There were some river willows growing out into the river on the other side. His body had floated with the currents and had settled among the trees.

This was not the relaxing day I had hoped for. It had started out really good, but when I think back to that day, I wonder: what on earth would I have done if I had hooked the man with my fishing line and drug him in. I don't even want to go there. That was the last time I

Recollections of Raven & Richlands

ever fished in the Dixon Hole. It was not because of what happened, but I have never had the chance to enjoy that experience since I left my Raven.

In a few days it was time to head out and become part of, "This Man's Navy." The recruiter picked me up early in the morning then on to Tazewell where we picked up a Mitchell man that was going to San Diego with me. Mitchell became a friend and would go to California, through boot camp and back to Tazewell County for boot leave in September. He would be a friend as we were in the same boat you might say.

After leaving Tazewell the recruiter motored to the West Virginia Turnpike and all the way to Ashland, Kentucky where we would hold up our right hand and take an oath given by an officer. It was official I was in the Navy. Next I was given my service number on a little strip of paper and given my first order. Recruit Whitt, you are to know this number when you get to your base in San Diego.

Then they loaded me and a few fellows up in a van and drove to the Tri-State Airport in Huntington, West Virginia. We flew to Cincinnati, Ohio where Mitchell and I changed planes to Los Angeles, California, then on to San Diego. We were greeted by a salty old Petty Officer with a vocabulary you wouldn't want to hear. We were taken to boot camp. And I survived it. I sure was glad to see the green mountains of Raven in late September 1964, on boot leave.

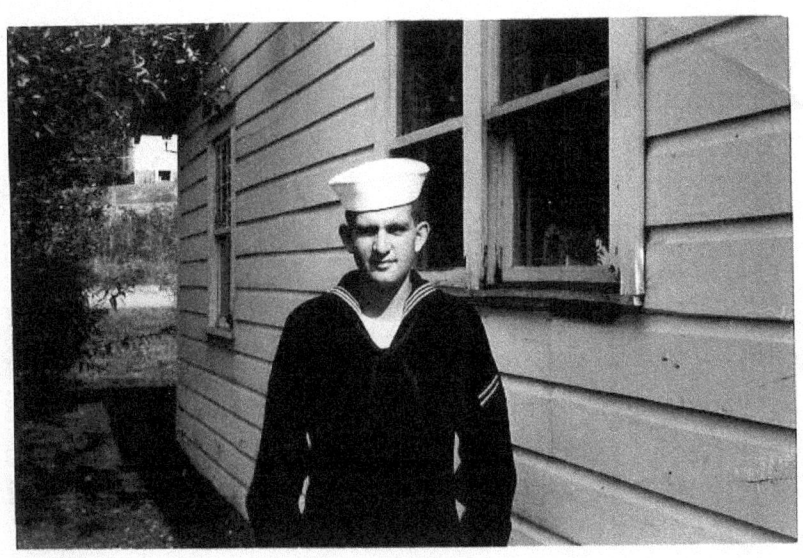

Home from boot camp September 1964

Chapter 24
Why I Love Raven & Richlands

As I think back to my childhood, I can think of many reasons why I love Raven, and Richlands, Virginia.

You may say that Raven is a dilapidated, dirty, little village and you would be partly right. If you look through a glass darkly, (coal dust) you would miss so much. Now look beyond the coal dust to the wonderful people that have lived and worked in Raven over the years.

Raven was once called the gateway to Buchanan County. Its mountains have given us many tons of coal and many board-feet of wood from its woods. These natural resources have made men rich but mostly it has given many little families a livelihood. Raven is a prime example of American culture, the rich and the poor living side by side.

I love Raven because of its rich tradition in the worship of the one true God that has created the universe and made a place like Raven. The churches around Raven are diverse but all have provided a place to worship and all promote Christian values. The churches and the schools of Raven have always taught the Golden Rule,

Colonel Charles Dahnmon Whitt

"Do unto others as you would have them do unto you." That is a wonderful rule to live by.

The people of Raven have learned to be thankful:

Thankful for the coal that God put under the mountains and the timbers that God put on the mountains.

Thankful for God making a place like Raven where it's isolation has held back great storms and the evilness of the great cities.

Thankful for their neighbors that are always ready to extend a hand to each other in time of need.

Thankful for the friendliness of Raven, where people still wave a passersby.

Thankful for Coal Creek, Hill Creek, Pine Creek, Mill Creek and the beautiful Clinch River.

Thankful for the natural beauty of the mountains and streams that the Creator of the Universe has given Raven.

Thankful for the deep white snows of winter.

Recollections of Raven & Richlands

Thankful for the green hills and shade of summer.

Thankful for the beauty of spring, the redbud and the dogwood decorate the hills and valleys.

Thankful for God's great art work in the fall when He paints the leaves so beautifully.

Thankful for the wonderful people that have lived in Raven and for those that still do. And for the pride they have because of their good will.

Thankful for the good old days and for the good tomorrows, Raven has kept it simple and honest.

Yes Raven has had its beer joints and some family feuds but the good has always outweighed the bad.

Have you ever seen the coal miners waiting for their rides to the mines in Raven? You will not see this in every little town. And have you seen the coal black faced angels when they get back from their day under the earth? There is no better feeling then having worked hard all day and accomplished a goal and earned a day pay, this is what these coal miners have always done. All the while they have flirted with death and danger

Colonel Charles Dahnmon Whitt

while doing their job.

Not many people in Raven have their Ph.D's but they are highly educated in what we call life. They have learned work, love of God, love of family, love of country, and community pride.

Just like in the Bible where there is a season for everything, nothing is for certain and things will change either better or worse. Raven has come through so many seasons, great and small and yet Raven is still there.

I am thankful that God made a place like Raven and put me there to grow up strong and true. I have a special feeling for the folks that have grown up in Raven. These people were there and people are there today that reflect the Golden Rule and peace and the pursuit of happiness.

There is a saying, it means something special, something different, something exciting, and for the folks of Raven, Virginia, Let's say we all have *"Gone Raven!"*
Oh! Let's also say, *"Go Blue Tornados"*

Recollections of Raven & Richlands

BOOM BUBBLE BURSTS

In 1892, when Cleveland was again elected President of the United States, the Philadelphia officials of the Clinch Valley Coal and Iron Company telegraphed their agents here to close down the mills and return to the Pennsylvania office.

Fred Raven, a bookkeeper for the company, and one of the Raven brothers for whom the village of Raven was named, was left in charge of the company's property. Not long afterward, Fred Raven, too, left and that was the end of the ambitious dream of the Clinch Valley Coal and Iron Company.

The Richlands Hotel, which, with its red plush carpeted floors, gas lights, private water works, crystal chandeliers, Dresden china, mahogany furniture, silver plate and service, equalled in extravagant splendor the present Waldorf Hotel in New York, was left deserted without even a caretaker. "Uncle Bob" Kitts recalls that the silver, goldcrusted china and other things were carried away by whosoever wanted it and, several years after the bubble burst and the ticking of the feather beds and pillows had rotted, he well remembered wading through feathers waist deep in some of the rooms.

There was no business in Richlands. Land and property was valueless. Most of the lots had been bought by Northerners who had vanished. Finally, lots which had originally sold for $1500 apiece, were sold for taxes for 25 cents or less; some were bought at tax sales for only three cents. It is reported that the company which was formed to acquire the holdings of the Clinch Valley Coal and Iron Company bought all the unsold lots in town for $1 apiece.

Taken From
1. *Tazewell County*
By: Louise Leslie
Pages 111, 150

Chapter 25
Sir Names

"Raven & Richlands has a rich Heritage in its people!"

I have made a list of some of the Prominent Surnames widely known in this area of southwest Virginia. If I left your name off it does not mean I left you off for any reason. It is that I just missed you by mistake. I know there must be many other names I failed to print.
Dahnmon

Recollections of Raven & Richlands

Absher,

Adair,

Adkins

Alicie,

Allen,

Altizer,

Arms,

Asbury,

Bailey,

Baldwin,

Bales,

Ball,

Bandy,

Barnett,

Baxter,

Beavers,

Belcher,

Bell,

Bishop

Blankenship

Boyd,

Breedlove,

Brewster,

Britts,

Brown,

Bryant,

Buchanan,

Busic,

Buskell,

Butcher,

Colonel Charles Dahnmon Whitt

Byrd,	Compton,	Deel,
Cantrell,	Cordill,	Dills,
Casey,	Cordle,	Dowdy,
Cassell,	Cox,	Dye,
Chaney,	Craig,	Elkins,
Childress,	Crawford,	Elswick,
Christian,	Crouse,	Evans,
Claypool,	Culbertson,	Farley,
Clines,	Cyphers,	Farmer,
Coleman,	Davis,	Ferrell,
Collins,	Davison,	Fields,

Recollections of Raven & Richlands

Fleming,	Hagy,	Hess,
French,	Hall,	Hicks,
Fugate,	Hankins,	Hill,
Fuller	Harman,	Hoban,
Gilbert,	Harris,	Hodge,
Gillespie,	Harrison,	Honaker,
Goodman,	Hawkins,	Horn,
Goodwin,	Hays,	Horton,
Green,	Helton,	Hubbard,
Greever,	Henderson,	Hunter,
Griffith,	Hensley,	Hurt,
Grose,	Herndon,	Hutchinson,

Colonel Charles Dahnmon Whitt

Jackson,	Kinder,	Mabe,
Jamison,	King,	Madden,
Jenkins,	Kiser,	May,
Jennings,	Lambert,	Maynard,
Jessee,	Lane,	McClanahan,
Johnson,	Lankford,	McCoy,
Jones,	Lawson,	McDowell,
Joyce,	Lester,	McGee,
Justice,	Lewis,	McGlothlin,
Keen,	Long,	McKenzie,
Kennedy,	Lowe,	McKinney,

Recollections of Raven & Richlands

Meadows,	Nunley,	Peterson,
Mercer,	Osborn,	Pierce,
Miller,	Owens,	Plaster,
Mitchell,	Pack,	Potter,
Monk,	Patrick,	Presley,
Muir,	Patterson,	Price,
Mullins,	Patton,	Proffitt,
Music,	Payne,	Pruitt,
Nash,	Pendelton,	Puckett,
Nelson,	Perkins,	Rasnake,
Newberry,	Perry,	Ratliff,
Null,	Persinger,	Ray,

Colonel Charles Dahnmon Whitt

Reed,	Salyer,	Stephenson,
Reedy,	Schrader,	Stevens,
Reeves,	Shaffer,	Stiltner,
Richardson,	Shelton,	Stilwell,
Ringstaff	Short,	Street,
Robinette,	Simmons,	Sullivan,
Robinson	Sizemore,	Sutherland,
Rose,	Skaggs,	Sword,
Russell,	Smith,	Sykes,
Rynolds,	Sparks,	Tabor,
	Stacy,	Tackett,

Recollections of Raven & Richlands

Tatum,	Warner,	Williams
Taylor,	Webb,	Williamson,
Thompson,	Welch,	Wilson,
Tizen,	Wells,	Winchester,
Tolliver	White,	Witt,
Turner,	Whited,	Witten,
Underwood	Whitt,	Wyatt
Vance,	Whitten,	Young,

Chapter 26

History of Richlands, by R.L. Crawford

R. L. CRAWFORD

History of Richlands

The Richlands Valley is in the extreme western part of the county. It has become one of the busiest and most extensive localities in Tazewell County. It has an area of 2 by 4 miles, or about five thousand acres of very valuable land. The most of it is bottom land and lies on the north and south side of Clinch River, which winds its way through the valley. From these fertile river lands the place receives its name. And in their midst is located the thriving and coming town of Richlands. The local and other industrial enterprises, including, primarily, coal operations, furnish a good market for most of the production of the small farmers.

The town of Richlands is located between two mountains; Sandy Mountain and Kents Ridge. It has limestone water on the south side and freestone water on the north side of the valley. Before being incorporated a town it was owned by the Barnes, who live at Tazewell.

In the year of 1888 the Clinch Valley Coal and Iron Company bought the lands of Richlands and started a town, which I will tell you all about in the future of this little book.

Richlands, located on Clinch River, 18 miles below Tazewell, 3 miles from county line.

It was a large farm owned by Gillespies. They were bought out by Clinch Valley Coal and Iron Company in 1889. The boom started early in 1888 and lasted for four years.

A Rolling Mill to make muck-bar iron from Pig Iron; a glass factory was built up Big Creek in north side of town but never operated. Glass blowers came to work in the glass factory and lived in "Glass Row" but the factory never operated. The puddlers came from far away Pennsylvania with their families. They lived in "Puddlers Row" and worked at the Rolling Mill for two years. Then it was closed down, March 18, 1894, wrecked and hauled away.

HISTORY OF RICHLANDS, VIRGINIA

The Clinch Valley Coal and Iron Company built the Street Bridge which still stands. The Richlands Hotel, on Washington Square, where Mattie Williams Hospital now stands, and the Griffiths House were burned.

A row of duplex houses above the Depot still stand; a row of houses on Lee Street, some still standing on both sides of the street. A row of houses on Glass Row, some of which are still standing. Ten double houses in Puddlers Row caught fire and all burned to the ground, several years after the boom.

The town went down for four years, until in 1897. Lots were high when the boom was on, but after the boom lots could be bought for from $1.00 to $25.00. Lots then sold for $25.00 that would now bring $2,000.00. One sale in west end lately brought $4,000.00 for four 25 ft. lots.

OFFICERS

The first 18 months the Town of Richlands had as officers two Baldwin-Felts detectives, and one Magistrate, or Esquire. In the year of 1891 (or near then) the Town was chartered as follows: January 26, 1892, the first elected mayor was William B. Spratt, on the Dry Ticket, elected by a 2-vote majority.

The first policeman was George Ratliff.

You would like to know why the town failed after the big boom. It was boomed by a big company that came here to boom this town for a speculation.

In the year of 1892 the presidential election was held, and Grover Cleveland was elected the second time.

March 18, 1894, the Rolling Mill was closed, and torn down and moved away.

They also shut down the glass factory, and turned it into a britter mill. That didn't pay and they tore it down, too.

In 1888 Gen. Harrison, Rep., was elected president of the United States. In the election of 1892, Grover Cleveland, Democratic party, with "Free Trade," was made president.

Iron made for 12½c a day. March 18, 1894, mills closed down.

In the Rolling Mill they took pig iron and made muckbar iron and shipped it away to finishing mills to be made into horse- shoes, wagon wheels, etc.

2

229

HISTORY OF RICHLANDS, VIRGINIA

The boom took place under Harrison. When the administration changed the panic began because of devaluation. The factories closed, no demand for bricks, glass or iron.

The town was so dead all it lacked being buried was just covering it up. The Railroad Company took up their track from Richlands to Seaboard. Their grade was used for a county road, to travel in, until H. Fugit built a tram road on it at the head of the creek, across the mountain and down to the foot of the mountain, known as Chicken Ridge, to a saw mill, and trucked the lumber out to the Glass Row to a car.

PIONEERS: Henry Shavnor, Louis Jones, Hewry Elswick, W. K. Hewson, A. S. Crawford, W. B. Spratt and Mrs. Spratt, A. C. Gardner and Mrs. Gardner, Teddy Clark, Tom Proffitt, J. B. Crabtree, R. L. Crawford, J. H. Brown, J. B. Lester, J. L. Hayden, Monsley Ratliff, D. Kitts, B. J. Ball, G. M. Brown, M. C. Greenburg, O. C. Duff.

EARLY DAYS IN RICHLANDS

LYNCHING— I remember the Negro lynching which took place on February 2, 1892. One of the darkest chapters in the town's history.

The way it started: Two men, Shortige and Ratliff came to Richlands from Buchanan County to get a load of goods to haul back to their county. While in Richlands they stepped into one of the saloons to buy a drink. There were two Negroes in the saloon, who watched the Buchanan County men and saw that they had money. Later the two men went back across the river to a sleight-of-hand show, on the second floor of the Hawkins & Beaners Building. (This building still stands a block west of the Street Bridge.) The Negroes followed the white men and learned where they would sleep that night, in the home of the widow Ratliff. Mrs. Ratliff lived in an old boarding house, (built as a commissary and boarding house, by Jim Scott, cross-tie man for the railroad.)

The Negroes way-laid the two white men when they left the show and started across the railroad track to Mrs. Ratliff's boarding house. W. K. Hewson's Negro driver, stealing a hatchet from the Hewson Dry Goods Store, with two or three other Negroes, way-laid the white men

3

HISTORY OF RICHLANDS, VIRGINIA

in the railroad cut, beating them with hatchets, robbing them, and left them for dead. Someone discovered the men and called George Ratliff, local policeman. Ratliff placed John Johnson, one of the Negroes, under arrest, who confessed and gave the names of his accomplices. Next morning deputy officers, A. S. Crawford and George Ages, started to Tazewell before daylight with Johnson to prevent the mob from taking him. The officers hid in the brushes and thickets of the forest, planning to flag the east bound passenger train, due at Cedar Bluff about 9 a. m. They waited for the train near the big curve above Cedar Bluff. The mob had gone west to a work train, down the valley, and seized two Negroes boarding the passenger train. The mob ordered the engineer and other trainmen at the point of a gun to do as they wished. They stopped at Richlands, searched the railroad station and not finding Johnson, boarded the train again, ordered the engineer to pull out, rode on to Cedar Bluff, stopped the train and searched the depot, not finding Johnson there, they boarded the train again and moved on through the big cut where they saw the two officers with the Negro prisoner. The train was halted and the mob came out of the train, fifty men or more, each with a gun. They said, "We'll take charge of this 'nigger'." They walked Johnson back to the west end of Richlands (now the brick yard section) to an old oak tree with a big limb. The Negroes were hung to the limb (three Negroes in all). Their hands were tied with rope to their legs, a rope was placed around their necks, placed on a horse, the rope thrown over the limb, and a man was up on the limb who tied the rope. Then the horse was led out from under the Negroes, one by one. While swinging the Negroes were shot at by the mob.

One Negro had been hung the night before, and the town authorities had cut him down and placed the body on a plank under the same tree. The dead body of the first mob victim lay under the tree while the blood-thirsty mob finished their job.

Old Johnson, while on the horse, confessed to killing Joe Hunt, of Pounding Mill, thus clearing the mystery of Joe Hunt's murder and robbery several years back. Johnson said that he and Sam Blow's son (colored) from Busthead,

4

HISTORY OF RICHLANDS, VIRGINIA

had robbed and killed Joe Hunt. Officers then arrested Blow's son, brought him to Richlands "calaboose", as the one room jail was called. In about one hour he was taken out of the calaboose by George Hankins, deputy sheriff. The Negro rode behind the sheriff, horse back, on the way to Tazewell court house. The mob followed and caught up with them above Cedar Bluff where they took the Negro from the sheriff and hung him to an apple tree beside the road.

Five were hung in that round, and more would have been hung, but the others hid from the mob. One Negro, Bill Tribulary, was hidden in a heating stove in the basement of the home of W. B. Spratt, for twenty-four hours.

HAPPENINGS - - - - - - - -

To show you that this town in its early days rivaled the "wild west", I will tell you a few of the things that happened during the 90's.

They would ride mules right up the board walk, bow heads down and ride right into a saloon. The saloon was soon empty—Everybody present would rush out the back door. Officers would come and take mule-back-riders out the door also.

A man by the name of Vince Wilson was mad at the town. He sent word that he was coming with his men to take the town. The town deputized several extra police. They sure enough came, and they started something. The officers tried to head them off at the Street Bridge, but Wilson's gang ran right through the officers and went up on the bank in front of the Hawkins Building and started shooting at the officers. They stood shooting until they were tired, and one officer got shot in the leg. Hubert Ranew was shot in the heel.

I remember another time when a man at Seaboard got mad at the town, and sent word that he would be down to take it Saturday night. The town deputized 25 extra police, and they arrived there. These officers started up the creek Saturday night to meet the Seaboard bunch, and they met them at the forks of Big Creek, opened fire on them, and shot and killed one man and wounded another. The rest of the gang went back toward Seaboard. They never made another attempt.

5

I remember another time that Jim Short killed a Negro in a restaurant (where bus station is now.) Jim Short was arrested, placed in the calaboose, but he kicked off a plank at the back side and escaped. As he ran across the bottom toward Brooklyn, he called back and said, "Your calaboose might hold flour but it wont hold Shorts." Later, he escaped into the woods and never came back.

After Jim's escape his brother was standing on the sidewalk, when John Wilson walked around in front of him and said, "Vance knows where Jim is and he's going after him."

Jim's brother said, "Vance had better let Jim alone."

John said, "No, he's gone after him."

About that time Short pulled out his knife and slashed Wilson across the bowels from one side to the other. Wilson, walking around holding his intestines up with his hands, begged for a doctor. Later, Dr. Williams fixed him up and he lived for many years.

I remember when Rans McGlothlin was an officer in Richlands. One afternoon he went to arrest a man on the street and the man resisted the officer and showed fight. They walked across the street and went behind the old theater, and opened fire on one another. The man was left-handed and the officer was watching the right hand, and the man shot the officer and the officer shot the man about the same time. They were both taken to the hospital and later both died.

WIFE CONFESSES TO MURDER OF HUSBAND AND DAVIS GIRL, JUNE 7TH, 1943

Mrs. Lula Freeman Bowling yesterday confessed to the slaying of 13-year-old Juanita Davis with an ax just before she killed her husband, D. J. Bowling, 39, with a shot gun, Monday, June 7, about 1:30 A. M., in their home on Kents Ridge.

Mrs. Bowling made her signed confession in the presence of Sheriff R. B. Thompson, Deputy Sheriff Dan C. Taylor, and Commonwealth's Attorney John W. Gillespie. She asked to talk to the sheriff about 12:30 A. M., Wednesday.

HISTORY OF RICHLANDS, VIRGINIA

She told officers she awoke shortly after 1 A. M., when her husband left their bed and went into the room of Juanita Davis, a neighbor girl who was a domestic helper in the Bowling home. She went into the kitchen and got an ax, slipped into the room and found her husband on the bed with the Davis child. She hit him with the ax and he rolled off the foot of the bed and went into the other room. She then struck Juanita over the head several times with the ax and followed her husband into their bedroom, where she said she tussled with Bowling for the shotgun, and grabbing it away from him, pulled the trigger. The blast blew the top of his head off.

Mrs. Bowling was taken into custody Monday morning and lodged in the county jail at Tazewell. Monday night she confessed to having killed her husband, charging that he had killed Juanita Davis with the ax. Upon returning to her room she said he had gotten the shotgun and told her to get their baby and they would all die together. She claimed to have tried to wrest the gun from him and in self defense had pulled the trigger.

Then she told the jailor's wife she wanted to talk to the sheriff, and made a complete confession of the murder of the Davis girl and her husband.

She will be arraigned for preliminary hearing before Trial Justice Albert G. Peery on June 16 at Tazewell.

Contrary to previous reports that Mrs. Bowling had called the Davis child's parents it now appears that the first alarm that all was not well at the Bowling home that night was realized when Juanita's grandfather, Bill Davis, heard the gun shot as he left Blair Davis's house where he had been to ask his son to go for a doctor because his wife was ill. Juanita's half-brother, James Shelton, a sailor, home on leave, said Monday that he was the first to arrive at the Bowling home after the alarm was sounded. He said that he discovered that Juanita was still breathing. Members of the family put the child in a truck to bring her to a Richlands hospital. She died enroute.

Juanita had worked for the Bowlings for about a week, going back and forth between that house and her parent's home which was about 150 yards away.

The Bowlings and their three-year-old son moved to Kents Ridge in April. They came to this section about

7

HISTORY OF RICHLANDS, VIRGINIA

four years ago from Kentucky. During this time Bowling had worked for various coal companies. At the time of his murder he was employed as a miner at Amonate.

Officers learned from his wife that he had deserted the army some years ago and had changed his name in an effort to escape discovery. Also there was a warrant out for his arrest in Kentucky.

DEATH OF MINER STILL CLOAKED IN MYSTERY

Mystery still surrounds the death of Orson Keene, of Shorts Gap, whose body was found about 5:30 on Saturday afternoon on the bank of Clinch River near The Topper, a road house on the Raven highway, just outside the corporate limits of Richlands.

His head battered in and his body badly decomposed when found, investigating officers said that he probably had been dead since Wednesday night. He had been struck near the left temple with a blunt weapon and his skull crushed.

County authorities are holding one man in the Tazewell jail as a material witness but no charges have been preferred to date.

Deputy Sheriff Dan Taylor, who has been active in the investigation, said he was inclined to believe Keene was killed in one place and then carried to the spot where his body was found. He is believed to have been in an altercation in a poker game Wednesday night which led to his death.

Keene and his wife were separated, according to officers. She went to the home of her mother, Mrs. Verlie Hunt, some weeks ago where he followed her and shot into the house. He was indicted on this charge and his trial was set for last Monday in Tazewell Circuit Court. Local officers do not believe the shooting has any connection with his death.

County officers are still at work on the case and it is expected that one or more suspects will be rounded up in the near future.

HISTORY OF RICHLANDS, VIRGINIA

CHURCHES

I remember the first church in Richlands. One room in the Hankins & Beavers Building was used for services. The first preacher we had was Rev. Woodrum, Methodist minister.

Now we have several churches in Richlands, namely: First Methodist, Presbyterian, Christian, Missionary Baptist, Union Church, Episcopal, and two Holiness churches.

The Methodist church came up through trial and hard times. It was paid for by small collections, by the faithful church members, namely:

A. C. Gardner and wife, Monsley Ratliffe and wife, W. B. Spratt and wife, W. P. Boggas and wife, George Bolley and wife, Old Brother Kitts, G. M. Brown, Mr. and Mrs. Farmer.

A lot more good old brothers and sisters, who stood together for right, that we can't remember at present.

HOSPITALS

The first hospital in Richlands was a small building, now used as a dental office and beauty shop, just back of the Williams house. Now we have two well equipped hospitals; the Mattie Williams, and Clinch Valley Clinic.

I remember the first amputation. It was down in the building now known as the Section House. In the room next to the Big Creek switch. I stood at the window and watched the doctor cut off a boy's leg which had been injured by a train.

I remember Dr. Williams operated on a young man for appendicitis, and while being carried on a stretcher to the house of Mrs. Graham Robinson, in the Brickyard Section, the patient woke up and jumped off the stretcher and started running away. He was caught and placed on the stretcher and tied there until he reached the home of Mrs. Robinson, who was a trained nurse.

We have first class treatment for patients at both the Mattie Williams Hospital and Clinch Valley Clinic now.

HISTORY OF RICHLANDS, VIRGINIA

BANKS

The first bank was in the stone building now occupied by the Richlands National Bank. Major Dunn of Abingdon, was the president of the first bank.

It was later moved to the present First National Bank building, and known as Merchants and Farmers Bank. It was organized in 1906. Dr. Williams was one of the first directors and elected first vice president. January 6, 1912, he was elected president of the bank and served in that capacity until the bank was changed from a State bank to the First National Bank of Richlands, in 1916. He became the first and only president of that institution, and he has lived to see the bank grow from $78,000 (records of 1908) to $2,000,000 (records of June, 1943.) Its deposits have steadily increased every year since its establishment.

Early in manhood Dr. Williams became interested in County and State politics. For years he was chairman of the Democratic Committee of Tazewell County.

A close friendship existed between him and the late Governor Stewart of Russell County. His brother-in-law, Geo. C. Peery, was elected to Congress in 1923, representing the Ninth district and was later elected governor of Virginia.

He built the Mattie Williams Hospital in 1915, on the site where stood the old Hotel Richlands, which after a brief time became the Old Dominion College. The frame building was torn away and handsome modern brick hospital was built. A large wing was added in 1936.

For the past 16 years his son, Dr. James P. Williams, has been closely associated with him in the hospital as surgeon-physician. In the fall of 1937 they expanded the hospital service to accommodate the Buchanan County patients nearer home by building and establishing the Grundy Hospital.

As a member of the State Board of Health, Dr. Williams worked for the expansion of public health of southwest Virginia.

THEATERS

I remember the first opera house in Richlands. It was in the old livery stable. Now, we have two modern theaters, thanks to Mr. Guy Flanary.

10

HISTORY OF RICHLANDS, VIRGINIA

WHOLESALE HOUSES

The first wholesale house was in the present location of the O K Restaurant. Now, we have two good wholesale houses; Dixie Grocery, and Marco Warner.

SCHOOLS

I remember the first school we had in Richlands. Two rooms on the second floor in the Hankins Building were used for school. Later Clinch Valley Coal & Iron Company built a four room brick building for the first school house. This building still stands on the present school grounds.

The first High school was taught in the old Hotel Richlands. It was a pay school. Professors Hutton and Kendrick of Honaker were the teachers.

Now we have as good Grade and High school buildings as are in the county. The first school bus that was put on the road in this town was owned and operated by R. L. Crawford. Since that time it has grown and takes about 8 or 10 buses to carry them to school from different parts of the county.

DEPOT AGENT

I remember the first depot agent in Richlands was a man by the name of Peters. He lived in the Dalton Addition. He built the old house that George Ratliff lived in, and then Dalton. It stood where the Allen McGuire brick house stands now. It was the first house to be built on that side of the river, and as well as I remember, Charlie Neel was the first telegraph operator that we had in Richlands.

OTHER ENTERPRISES

The first transfer trucks in Richlands were owned by Frank West and Patsy Warner.

The first brick plant in Richlands was out where Bill Hankins owns at this time. It was a little press brick plant, with a capacity of about 30,000 bricks a day. When

11

HISTORY OF RICHLANDS, VIRGINIA

the boom went down the railroad took up the track back to the main line and piled up the steel. Now we have one of the best shale brick plants in the southwest. It has a capacity of about 150,000 bricks per day.

The first silversmith was a man by the name of S. M. Trial. He lived in Brooklyn.

I'll never forget his motto he put in his watches: Wind me with care, and treat me well, and I to you the time will tell, and if by chance I should fail, take me back to S. M. Trail.

And for the last several years we have had the best silversmith in the State. His name is J. L. Haden, who is still here, and his daughter is his assistant.

The first undertaker was B. F. Ball. He had a small hearse, drawn by horses. He kept this business for a couple of years, then Billy Farmer settled here, and worked for the R. R. Co. Because of ill health he quit the R. R. Co., and gave all his time to the undertaking business. Mr. Farmer had a hearse drawn by horses, and he has made a successful business up to date.

His son took over and is now a successful and good undertaker.

I remember the first piano that was shipped to this town. My father and I hauled it on a sled with two yoke of cattle and put it in Henry Shannon's home on Tank Hill, now owned by Duffs.

The first water system we had in this little town was up above Hadens, in a pump house which pumped the water around the hill. The second water system was down where the bridge goes to the Dalton Addition, which was owned by Clark & Davy. Clark & Davy also put in the first lighting system in this town. All through the 90's we didn't have any street lights. Now we have the best water and lighting systems in southwestern Virginia. Our water is from a spring which is across the ridge, 2½ miles from town.

The first printing office we had here was owned by G. G. Harris. He printed a paper of about 12 inches square. Now we have two as good printing offices as any in the county.

The first postmaster of Richlands was W. K. Houston.

HISTORY OF RICHLANDS, VIRGINIA

SALOONS OF THE 90'S

Ira Alley, across from depot; Jerry Carter, where Easley Florist Shop is now; a saloon where the present A.B.C. store now stands; on the corner below W. F. B. White's Hardware store was another saloon and boarding house, a three-cornered, two-story building, known as the "Black Mari"; a saloon in a small yellow building near the Rexall Store; and also a saloon where the Rexall Drug Store now stands, which was operated by Jake Lickensteen and M. C. Greenburg. And in the year of 1935 there was a dispensary established on Main Street, controlled and operated by the government.

I have tried to give you the history of our little town. I can't explain to you how bad this country was during the 90's. Men used to come to town from the surrounding country and with their pistols hanging to their sides. When they would leave town they would start shooting, and the town officers couldn't do much with them. Some of these men are still living, but they are much better men.

I want to say that we have a town made up of first class citizens, and we have as good and modern little town as there is in the southwest.

As I have given you the history of our little town, I will now list some of the conveniences of the town:

Good citizens; good churches; 2 funeral homes; 2 hardware stores; 2 banks; 1 first class post office; 2 hospitals; 2 theaters; a good water and lighting system; 1 casket factory; 1 brick yard; 7 drygoods stores; 9 grocery stores; 2 printing offices; 2 wholesale houses; 1 A.B.C. store, 7 restaurants; 3 barber shops; 4 beauty shops; 2 dental offices; 3 garages; 2 radio shops; 1 recapping shop.

We also have 10 doctors, namely: Drs. Parsons and Cunningham, local doctors; Dr. J. A. Obercombe, chief surgeon and at present head of the hospital staff at Mattie Williams Hospital. Dr. Philip W. Orden, surgery and urology; Dr. W. R. Strader, medicine and obstetrics; Dr. Joe B. Pantera, eye, ear, nose and throat specialist—all of Mattie Williams Hospital.

Dr. J. A. Robinson, medical doctor; Dr. N. G. Patterson, surgeon; Dr. A. D. Parsons, medical interest; Dr. E. H. Kirk, eye, ear, nose and throat specialist; Dr. G. D. Vermel, of the local staff, now in the service—All of the Clinch Valley Clinic.

13

HISTORY OF RICHLANDS, VIRGINIA

To my knowledge the town was developed by this group of good citizens, namely:

Dr. W. R. Williams, W. B. Spratt, W. B. F. White, J. B. Crabtree, A C. Gardner, W. P. Boggess, C. C. Hyatt. W. P. Farmer, W. E. Mullins, T. A. Draper, R. L. Lambert, Joe Brown, O. F. Brown, C. B. Orr, Ballard Elswick, Reece Serber, J. B. Lester, Al McGuire, John Draper, Albert Buskell, Elick Buskell, M. M. Hankins, P. Davis, G. M. Brown, Teddy Clark, Edd Clark, Robert West, Walter Cordwell, Roy White, I. T. Jessee, John Joyce, Claude Helton, Lon Kelley, I. E. Horton, Guy Flanery, Mac Greenburg, Johnnie Burton, Billie Fields.

And now we have a population in and around Richlands of about 4,000 people.

THE TOWN OF RICHLANDS

There is a town called Richlands,
   On the Banks of the "River Smile,"
Where the cheer up and be happy
   Blossoms sweetly all the while.

Where they never crumble flowers
   Beside the fragrant try;
And they never give up patients—
   Point their faces toward the sky.

In the valley of old Clinch River—
   In the PROVINCE of I WILL,
You will find this lively city
   At the foot of "No Fret Hill."

There are.......................delightful
   In this very charming town;
And on every hand there are shade trees
   Amid the very seldom frown.

Rustic benches, quite enticing,
   You'll find scattered here and there,
And to each a vine is clinging—
   Called the frequent, earnest prayer.

Everybody there is happy—
   And is singing all the while;
In the town of old Richlands—
   On the banks of "River Smile".

14

HISTORY OF RICHLANDS, VIRGINIA

WHAT DADDY SAID

When I first came to Richlands
    I didn't come to stay—
I had no money
    And I couldn't get away.

Daddy said, be quiet son,
    For you will live to see
Richlands come to the front,
    And it will better be.

When men would come alone,
    With guns hanging by their side,
It scared me so
    I almost cried.

Daddy said, be quiet son,
    For you will live to see
Richlands come to the front,
    And it will better be.

Then I tried to content myself—
    I thought I'd live to see
Richlands—which is a better town
    Than I thought it would be.

Daddy said, be quiet son,
    I knew you would live to see
It is a better town
    Than you thought it would be.

The writer of this little history, a boy who came to this town at the age of 17 years, in the year of 1888, is now 75 years old. He came here before this was a town. He came with his father, A. S. Crawford, from Smyth County to live, and has been a citizen in and around Richlands for the past 59 years.

                              R. L. CRAWFORD

Written in 15 1946

RAVEN-1914 GATEWAY

Raven, in 1914 was called "the gateway to Buchanan County", and the "outlet for coal and lumber from the mountains to the north." All travelers from Tazewell into Buchanan went by Raven since the main road to Grundy was built across the mountains, coming out at this point, where it intersected with other roads. Nearly every lawyer now living and practicing here, as well as others of years ago—saddle bags lawyers—traversed this historic pike across the ridges to Grundy to attend court. Now, since the railroad has been built from somewhere on the Elkhorn up to within about 9 miles of Grundy, lawyers and other important and less important visotors go that way instead of following the old trail across the mountains from Raven, on horseback. Gone are the old taverns and stopping places of years ago, where the lawyers, wagoners, and other stopped to "feed" at noon, or to spend the night, and where, it is said, an appetizing nip of "Applejack" could always be had if you happened not to have the same in your saddle-pockets and as good a meal as was ever spread of the best the country afforded.

Major Henry, Judge Graham, Judge Stuart, Judge Coulling, and other lawyers have made the welkin ring with their eloquence in other days, and do yet, on occasions. Some great legal battles have been fought in the humble court house at Grundy by some of the strongest lawyers in the State, over land titles and other causes of litigation.

By: Louise Leslie

Colonel Charles Dahnmon Whitt

Chapter 27

Our First Television

Long about 1951 or 1952 we started hearing about the marvel called Television. It was a box that had sound like a radio, but added a moving picture and was instantaneous.

We lived in the mountains and knew we could get lots of radio stations at night, but not too many in the daytime. We all wanted a Television but knew there had to be a special antenna put in a good spot to receive the picture. We kids and mom urged Dad to take the special offer from the Raven Super Market, which was a trial period. They would bring you a Television set and antenna and if you could get a station and wanted it you could keep the TV and pay for it.

Dad agreed to try it and had June Horton get us a TV and dad got it all hooked up. They turned the antenna every which way but loose, but could only get one channel and it was snowy. The station was in Roanoke, VA.

Recollections of Raven & Richlands

Our friends, Rosco and Nanny Bell Young came down to see our new television. Rosco said if he could get a picture that good he wanted a TV. The Youngs lived up on the ridge above us so dad figured they could get it even better. Today you would call this crazy, but in 1952, it was something wonderful to own a TV and get one channel.

Bluefield, WV was building a Television station and would be broadcasting soon so Dad decided to keep the set.

Soon Bluefield was on the air part time and we got a fair picture. At first the new station was just on for a few hours and most of the programing was movies of World War II.

Later the real programing started with Skoop and Snopp, Howdy Doody, Cisco and Pancho. Oh yes we were getting big time shows and news with Chet Huntley and David Brinkley and oh yes a new thing called Soap Operas.

My Dad heard of antenna boosters and Jacob's ladder TV wire. It was a Thanksgiving weekend I think, that

Colonel Charles Dahnmon Whitt

Dad put a new bigger antenna on McGlothlin's hill. He had the new antenna and rolls of Jacob's ladder wire and the electric booster. Now let me tell you about Jacob's ladder TV wire. It was 2 strands of wire and held apart about every 8 inches by a piece of plastic that resembled a ladder. The coils of wire put together could just about reach Heaven I think.

We were all ready, Dad would put the antenna up on the high hill and station us boys just at shouting distance apart and mom would watch the TV. After all was hooked up to suit Dad, we were ready. There must have been one thousand feet of Jacob's ladder wire ran out from the house across the creek, across the dirt road, up the steep hill. We were all stationed and dad hollered to Jerry, "How is that?"

Jerry hollered to Larry, "How is that?

Larry turned down the steep hill and hollered at me, "How is that?" I turned to the open window where Mom was watching for a good picture. I hollered toward the house, "How is that?"

Mom Hollered back at me, "Turn it."

I hollered loud as I could back to Larry, "Turn it."

Larry turned toward Jerry and hollered toward Jerry, "Turn it."

You get the picture? Well, we didn't, even though Dad turned that Antenna every which way but loose and we hollered at each other for hours.

The picture was just as good on top of the house in Stinson Bottom.

It was a fun day for me, putting out all that Jacob's ladder wire and listening to all the hollering.

Well in a few days Dad took it all down and put the antenna back on the house. He even carried it all around the yard looking for the best picture.

I think it was way up in the sixties before Dad could get cable TV run to the house. Then came the color TV. Most of them had a round screen. And the color was not too good.

That was TV in the good old days.

Colonel Charles Dahnmon Whitt

Chapter 28

Some Old Pictures

This Marker still stands today!
It is at the opening to the Clinch Valley Memorial Cemetery

Recollections of Raven & Richlands

Raven Drug Co. 1963

Colonel Charles Dahnmon Whitt

Raven Drug Co. March 2013
It was just Slammed by a big truck

Recollections of Raven & Richlands

Heading out of Raven on the old Rout 460 East

Colonel Charles Dahnmon Whitt

The Raven Super Market as seen in 2013

Heading toward Short's Gap through Old Raven, Old Route 460

This old building served as the Raven Post Office for many years.

Recollections of Raven & Richlands

Richlands Florist 1950's Van

Colonel Charles Dahnmon Whitt

Richlands Police in 1972
4th from left, front row, Officer Jack Young, he became and served as Police Chief for many years.

Reflection of the times — The Star Theatre, located on Front Street near where Cindy's Style Boutique is now located, once was a popular draw. When this photo was taken in the early 1940s, 'Scattergood Baines' was playing.

Colonel Charles Dahnmon Whitt

Cury's was a well know clothing store for many years in Richlands. It was last ran by Rod Cury.

Colonel Charles Dahnmon Whitt

The First Day

JULY 20, 1946

SOMETHING NEW HAS BEEN ADDED - THE NYLON LINE-Last Saturday morning Richlanders line up with the rest of the nation to get Nylon stockings, a special feature of the opening of D. Cury's new department store on Front Street. Taken just after the opening time at 9 o'clock, the picture above shows a part of the crowd which gathered at the door. At one time the line reached to Rexall Store at the end of the block.

Recollections of Raven & Richlands

Can you remember when Richlands was this busy?
It was this busy every Saturday Morning in the Early 1950's.

Colonel Charles Dahnmon Whitt

Birdseye View, Richlands, Va., looking Northeast.

Look at near the center to see the Grand Old Hotel "Richlands"

Recollections of Raven & Richlands

Hotel Richlands, a lavish inn built to temporarily house investors and their guests in the early 1890's. It stood on the site of the Mattie Williams Hospital on Washington Square.

Colonel Charles Dahnmon Whitt

This is the 1951 Riclands High School Band

The forerunner of the big new hospital that is there today.

Colonel Charles Dahnmon Whitt

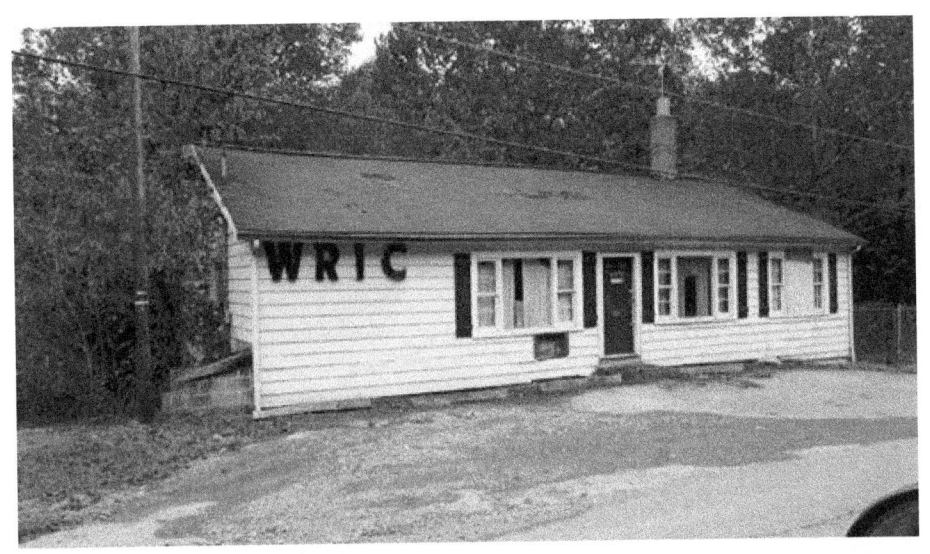

This little 1000 Watt AM radio station reached Farther than any other 1000 Watt station. It was known as the most powerful 1000 watts in the Nation.

Recollections of Raven & Richlands

Our Moms all saved S & H Green Stamps

Colonel Charles Dahnmon Whitt

The Old Esso Station at Claypool Hill
Don't know Bill!

Recollections of Raven & Richlands

Looking toward House and Barn Mountain

From Claypool Hill

Colonel Charles Dahnmon Whitt

Richlands had two theaters I remember, Flanary and Star, plus a Drive-in theater called Guy's

W. B. F. White & Sons

Colonel Charles Dahnmon Whitt

Across from Richlands High.

King Kone Now 2013

Next one was then.

Colonel Charles Dahnmon Whitt

King Kone 1965 Then!

Recollections of Raven & Richlands

Doran between Raven and Richlands

Colonel Charles Dahnmon Whitt

Brother Larry Worked here. Everyone got their cars here.
They even sold refrigerators.

Recollections of Raven & Richlands

Old Days

SUFFOLK AVENUE, RICHLANDS, VIRGINIA

Colonel Charles Dahnmon Whitt

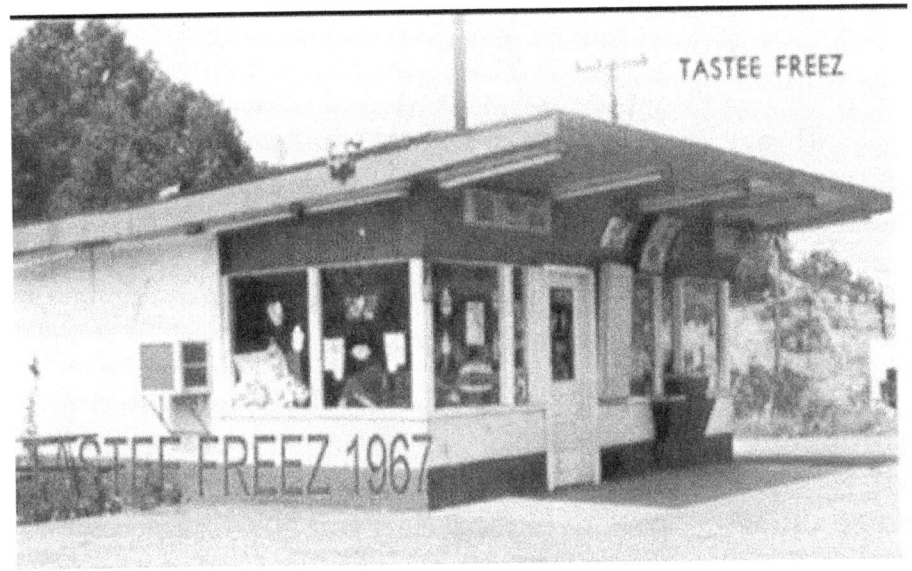

It Was Across From Richlands High School

Chapter 29
Our First Telephone

I am not sure how old I was, but I was in school when Dad and Mom decided to get our first telephone. It was a great adventure to me to have a machine like that in our house. We could pick it up get the operator and call around the world that is if you could get on. It was what they call a party line and most of the time someone was on it and even having a party. You could listen to every word so you had to watch what you said. I think about eight families were on our party line. If you wanted to call you may have to ask another party to get off long enough to make that call.

How did we know if we got a call, because it rang all the time? Each party had a different ring. I mean it may be three longs and a short or any combination. It reminded you of Morse code. I don't remember what our ring was, but I remember our telephone number. It was 855W4. My aunt Elsie that lived in Worthington KY had a number I remember. It was OAK413.

After a period of time Mom allowed me to make some calls. I remember the first girl I ever called. It was my bus riding friend later on. Her name was Linda Boyd and she lived up on the ridge above us. It is now called Young Road.

Think of the progress since then. From the old party lines to dial phones and private lines, to pushbutton calling to cell phones. Now we walk around with smart phones that take pictures, send messages and act as a computer.

I never dreamed that people could walk around with tiny telephones and call all over the world with a few little clicks.

I think that Alexander Graham Bell would flip over in his grave if he could see the evolution of his telephone.

Chapter 30
Power Lawn Mowers

Bet you thought lawn mowers always had motors. Wrong, we had the push models when I was a boy. They were hard to push if you let the grass get too high. I remember I mowed the lawn when I got big enough to push that thing. We had one patch of grass on one side of our house that was well watered and had plenty of sun. It was just too tough for me and Dad always cut it if I did the rest.

The first lawn mower with a motor I ever saw belonged to a farmer, Bill Nash. He had a rotary mower that he mounted a gasoline engine to. I thought it was special. Bill was a private person so I never got to see it up close but admired it from afar.

Then my neighbors the Kennedy's got a power mower that you pushed but it had a spinning blade on the bottom that cut the grass and threw it out the side. Kenny Kennedy got the job of cutting my grandmothers grass. That thing was amazing. Soon Dad got one of his own. My work was easier except with the new concept mower, we added so much more to our grass cutting area.

Then and Now.

Chapter 31
S & H Green Stamps

Anyone that lived through the fifties and sixties in the Richlands area can remember collecting S & H Green Stamps and maybe others like Top Value Stamps.

During this era of time certain merchants offered the trading stamps as an incentive to buy from them. According to how much you spent determined the number of stamps you received. The stamps were sought after by most mothers that did the most of the shopping. They were held in high regard because the stamps could be redeemed for nice prices.

The S & H Green Stamp company issued a catalog and blank books to paste in your stamps. After books were filled with the green stamps they could be taken to an exchange store and the prize you picked out could be yours. The only thing it often took many books to get anything. The S & H stamp store we went to was about 50 miles from Raven, it was located in Bluefield.

Some merchants would even offer double stamps in some situations. This really brought in the business.

The whole family took part in the collection and my job was to lick them and stick them in the books. Sometimes the redeemed prize was for me, Dad, or my brother, but mostly the articles traded were household items. Everyone felt like they were getting something for nothing, but I am sure the stamps drove up the items people shopped for. Yet it was fun and something to do.

I venture to say that the trade stamps spurred the economy and made folks feel better. Reckon we should bring them back?

Chapter 32

WRIC

I talked a little about my grand pa's old radios back in Grand Parents chapter. Now I will talk just a little bit about a slightly more modern era.

I remember our radio station fondly. I can even remember when they built it. I was just a little kid but WRIC AM radio was our station.

Let me say a few words about radio before I say much about WRIC. I remember when I was just little both my Grandpas had a large stand up cabinet radio and these old radios could pick up signals all over the world.

These radios were in most households and very important to the families. These radios required an antenna or aerial as some were called. These aerials were nothing more than a wire stretched resembling a clothes line.

The families would gather around the old radios and the world came into their living rooms. The news of WW I

Colonel Charles Dahnmon Whitt

WW II, Korea, and many other disasters came through the old radios. Much needed entertainment such as the Grand Old Opera and the Big Bands like Glenn Miller. There was sports shows like baseball and even horse racing , and oh yes "Serials" like Laurel and Hardy, Red Rider, The Lone Ranger, Amos & Andy, The Shadow and many more.

Of course there were commercials on the radio, tooth paste to long john underwear to cigarettes. There were many jingles to catch the ear, one that came to mind is "You will wonder where the yellow went when you brush your teeth with Pepsodent."

Finally we had our Radio Station, it was WRIC AM and it was built on Edgewater Drive between Richlands and Cedar Bluff. The tall antenna was built there also instead of on one of the mountains. Funny thing was the little 1000 watt station reached out so far that the station got a name as being the most powerful 1000 watts in the nation.

I remember we were on a trip to Worthington, KY in my Dad's 1959 Pontiac which had a "Wonder Bar" radio.

Recollections of Raven & Richlands

We picked up Richlands WRIC in Ashland, KY. Now it was not real good from that 200 mile distance but none the less we could listen.

I remember much about the little station as I grew up. It was only on the air from Sunrise to Sunset so we said it got us up and put us to bed. It came on the air with the playing of the National Anthem and signed off with the old song, "Come home, come home, its supper time!"

The music they played was mostly country and blue grass, but a time was set aside to play a more pop type music.

They had preaching and gospel music and also kept us abreast of the current obituaries. My Mom always listened to see who died and after listening she would say, well I'm not on there; guess I ain't dead yet and she would laugh.

I remember in the 2nd and 3rd grades we kids would buy one post card that cost a penny. We would address it to WRIC and then request a song we wanted to hear. Then all of us would sign our names. We would mail it at the Raven Post Office and listen each day when they

Colonel Charles Dahnmon Whitt

read requests and played songs. Sure enough, they would play our song and even mention every one of our names. We thought that was so cool to hear our names on the radio.

Transistors hit the market in around 1959 and by replacing the big vacuum tubes it was possible to build tiny radios not much bigger than a pack of cigarettes.

The Christmas of 1959 many kids got one of the new tiny radios. They only picked up AM as FM was not out yet.

I will always remember WRIC with fondness.

Chapter 33

Air Conditioning

Now in the highlands of the Clinch Valley area of SW Virginia it almost always cools down quickly when the sun goes down. Very few folks or even business had air conditioning in the fifties or even the sixties. We all felt safe just opening our windows and let the breezes blow through to cool us down. Most folks never even locked the doors and often left it open during the hottest times. Window screens were often used to keep out the bugs.

I do remember that the Britts that owned and ran the Raven Drug Company had a big window air conditioner pretty early. One time it went down and there were no one to fix it. My Dad, Marvin Whitt was often called to work on water pumps and other house hold machinery. Jack Britts knew this and had dad come and look at his Air Conditioning unit. Dad told him he had never worked on one before, but Jack insisted that Dad come and look at it. Sure enough Dad fixed it. I don't know the details but I know Dad was good at fixing things.

Colonel Charles Dahnmon Whitt

I have to tell you a little story about a traveling business man coming through Raven in the early fifties. I think he was driving a new Cadillac and it was one of the first cars to have air conditioning.

Most folks did their cars like they did their houses, they put down the windows in hot weather. We had a saying 4-50 system which meant, four windows down and run 50 miles per hour to keep cool.

Now the business man came through on an exceptionally hot day, and he noticed a boy walking and carrying some things for the farm. The business man pulled over and asked the boy if he wanted a ride. The boy was glad to catch a ride so he jumped in the new Cadillac. The windows were up and a cold breeze hit the boy in the face but he never said anything.

Next the business man struck up a conversation and asked the boy what the folks on the farm were doing on a day like this. The boy politely answered, "Well pa and my brothers were working in the field when I left, but since this Northerner has blowed in, they may be killing hogs."

Chapter 34

Killing Hogs

In my early years most country folks in the region would build a hog pen and house and get themselves a pig to fatten up. This was one way of making sure the family had plenty of meat and lard to sustain them through most of the coming year.

Now if you had a boar it had to be cut, or neutered, to make the meat better. Now once my friend Doug and I had to hold down two good sized pigs while Doug's dad, Checker did the deed.

Lordy, I thought those pigs were going to eat me up so I held with all my might. Finally after the 'Mountain Oysters" were removed from the pigs and medicine applied we turned loose and got out of the way. I felt sorry for the pigs, but knew it had to be done.

Dad was like most folks and always raised a pig to a huge fattened hog. Back then before they invented "Cholesterol" the fatter the hog the better.

Colonel Charles Dahnmon Whitt

Folks would save table scraps and grow corn to feed the hogs, often "Hog Chop" was added if needed. Hog Chop was a Powderly substance produced by feed companies and was always packaged in print material so the ladies had dress making material. The hog chop I think was chopped fodder and corn.

The hogs loved to root around and lay in the mud if possible. Most folks made a low place in the pen so the hogs could have mud. I have found that hogs will eat most anything from acorns, to even human flesh. After the battle of Cold Harbor in the Civil War, it was reported that hogs came out of the woods at night and fed on the poor Union Soldiers left in the killing field.

I remember us boys often had the chore of slopping the hogs and that just about describes feeding the hogs. There was always a hog trough made out of boards in the shape of a "V" and that was where the slop was poured in. The hogs always managed to get it all even in the deep crack of the trough.

When cold weather hit folks would be ready to kill hogs. It happened around Thanksgiving most of the time.

Recollections of Raven & Richlands

Sometimes neighbors would help, sometimes a hired hand would be employed. I remember a good man that hired out to kill hogs or in spring he would bring his team of horses and plow gardens. His name was Herman Lawson and he was well respected for his good work.

I want to stray for a minute and tell you one little story about Herman. There was a big hill from the old White Church all the way down into Stinson Bottom where a narrow wooden bridge crossed Mill Creek. Herman was coming down the hill in his wagon and his horses ran away. It was utter chaos and the horses missed the bridge turning the wagon upside down in the creek on top of Herman. I think several people went to his rescue and believe it or not neither the horses nor Herman were hurt bad, just shaken.

Now most folks used a 22 caliber rifle to put down the hogs, some were, like Herman's a sawed off version.

Colonel Charles Dahnmon Whitt

The hog would be given some food and the rifle was put between the eyes of the hog and usually one shot did it. Down with a crash would go the giant hogs. Next the hog would be hoisted up by rope or chain and his throat would be cut and the blood would be drained. I can't remember, but in the process there would be a barrel slanted over with water and a fire to heat it. This was done to soak the hog in real hot water to make it easy to remove the hair. Of course the guts were removed in here somewhere. Some folks saved the guts to be made into "Chitlins". I really didn't like to see this part.

The women would be ready with big fires and kettles to render the lard from the fat of the hog. The by-product would be cracklings or meat skins

I remember some neighbor boys always got the bladder and blew it up and used it for a ball.

Recollections of Raven & Richlands

The first fruits of the hog killing would be the tender loin. It was better than Ham or chops, Ummmm so good!

Dad would sugar cure the hams and shoulder with a giant needle and shoot some mixture into the meat. Then he would salt it all down and lay it in the smoke house.

Most folks kept chickens also. This supplied eggs and fryers for Sunday dinners.

I hated the chickens for one reason. I always went barefooted in the summer. Yes I would get chicken shit between my toes.

Chapter 35

Busy Richlands

In the chapter, "Old Pictures," there is an old picture of the business of Richlands in the nineteen fifties. I think it was 1954 and on Saturdays when all the folks came to town it was like a big city.

Back then there were no Malls or Walmart's. Folks came to town for several reasons, to shop at the various stores and one big reason was to socialize with friends. Sometimes meeting were set to do paper work for mining or other ventures like trading cars. Everybody had needs and wants in Richlands on Saturday.

The Farm Bureau, had things related to farming, Cury's Department Store had fine clothing for the entire family, the food stores kept the things folks didn't raise, and there were even jewelry stores to purchase wedding rings, and watches. People gassed up their cars and trucks at around .20 cents a gallon.

Now back then there were no one way streets as there is now. I kid you not, it took thirty minutes to an hour to get through Richlands.

Chapter 36

Haircuts

The first haircuts I remember getting came from Dad. I had long blonde curls of baby hair and Dad was ready for me to look like a boy. He caught Mom gone and gave me a short boy's haircut. The blond curls never did come back. That was the story told to me as I don't remember the first, but I sure remember many after that.

Dad had hair clippers that were manual, with no electric motor. They remind you of grass trimmers with a hair cutting head. The reason I remember these haircuts was those hand clippers. I think they pulled out about as much hair as they cut. Every time dad squeezed the handles together, the cutters on the head moved back and forth, only thing they pulled hair as well as cut. I was really glad when I could go to the barber Charlie Jackson or Henry Whitt and get my hair cut. I think it was .75 cents to get your hair cut. I loved the electric clippers, no more pulling.

Recollections of Raven & Richlands

Manual Hair Clippers

Chapter 37

Ball Point Pens

Can you remember when there were No Ball Point Pens? I remember when I saw my first ball point pens. I was in the Second grade at Raven School up on the hill. It had to be 1951 or 1952.

A salesman came to the school and gave all us kid's two ball point pens to take home and sell. I guess the school would get a cut from the sales, but don't know.

The thing I remember most was that the whole class found out how to click the pens top to make the point come out and go in.

I don't remember how many pens were sold or if any made it back in one piece. When we got them the whole class was going, click, click, click!

The teacher had all she could stand and made us put them away.

Recollections of Raven & Richlands

Colonel Charles Dahnmon Whitt Sr.

Raised in Raven, VA

Colonel Charles Dahnmon Whitt

Colonel Whitt a native of Raven in Tazewell County. Colonel Whitt attended High school in Richlands High School, Richlands, VA. He is a Vietnam War Veteran and served in the U.S. Navy. He moved to Kentucky in 1970 to carry out his trade as a Sheet Metal Worker with Local 24, Southern Ohio. Although he is now retired, he has always had an interest in genealogy and was always a real history buff for regional and civil war history; however, he didn't pursue his interest until he started researching his ancestry on-line in 1999.

While tracing his family's heritage, Whitt was soon introduced to his great-grandfather David Crockett Whitt. Yes, the discoveries that he had made during his fascinating search led him to create **"Legacy, The Days of David Crockett Whitt,"** a work of historical fiction with his great-grandfather serving as the skeleton for this account of life in an earlier, and harder time 1836-1909.

Legacy follows Colonel Whitt's great-grandfather "Crockett," through the early settler days in Virginia and Kentucky from 1836 thru 1909, his formative years in Greenup County Kentucky, War years as a Confederate, and the time that he spent in a Union Civil War prison.

Colonel Whitt has now written another book, **"The Patriot, Hezekiah Whitt,"** which deals with the years of 1760 -1846. Hezekiah Whitt was a founding father of Tazewell County, Virginia. He was a Militiaman, Indian Spy, Sheriff, and a lifelong Gentlemen Justice of the Peace appointed by the Governor of Virginia. Hezekiah Whitt is Colonel Whitt's GGG Grandfather. His bride was an Indian Maiden and the daughter of the great Shawnee War Chief, Cornstalk. This book abounds with Indian stories.

In **"Legacy, The Days Of David Crockett Whitt"** and **"The Patriot, Hezekiah Whitt"** you will soon discover when acquainting yourself with these particular titles is that Colonel Whitt encompasses his Christian faith and shows these pioneer families relying on their faith as well to get through trying times.

Charles is able to use the prefix "Colonel" in his pen-name because he is a Kentucky Colonel.

Other books by Colonel Charles Dahnmon Whitt Sr.

The Patriot, Hezekiah Whitt

Legacy, The Days of David Crockett Whitt

Colonel Charles Dahnmon Whitt

Legacy 2nd Edition

Dahnmon's Fantastic Dream

Haunts And Spirits Of The Past

Dahnmon's Little Stories

Confederate American

The South Won, What If?

Life's Journey

Gone Raven

Recollections Of Raven And Richlands

You can find all of these books at: http://dahnmonwhittfamily.com/ or on Amazon.com and other fine book dealers. Also Amazon offers the books as E-Books that you can down-load to your Kindle or PC.
 For a signed book, call 606-836-7997 for information!
 E-mail c-dahnmon@roadrunner.com

www.ingramcontent.com/pod-product-compliance
Lightning Source LLC
Chambersburg PA
CBHW051039160426
43193CB00010B/997